Beyond Harvard

**ALL-NEW STREET SMARTS FROM THE
WORLD OF MARK H. McCORMACK**

Beyond Harvard

ALL-NEW STREET SMARTS FROM THE
WORLD OF MARK H. McCORMACK

Edited by Jo Russell

PROFILE BOOKS

First published in Great Britain in 2017 by
Profile Books Ltd
3 Holford Yard
Bevin Way
London WC1X 9HD
www.profilebooks.com

A CIP catalogue record for this book is available from the British Library.

ISBN 978 1 78125 699 2
eISBN 978 1 78283 282 9

Text design by Sue Lamble
Typeset in Minion by MacGuru Ltd
Printed and bound by CPI Group (UK) Ltd,
Croydon, CRO 4YY

Dedicated to our father, Mark Hume McCormack, and his many friends and colleagues who are keeping his legacy alive.

The McCormack family

Contents

Foreword

Mark H. McCormack invented sports marketing as we know it today. His vision and genius changed the world of sport – and the lives of those who play it, watch it and love it – forever. By linking the celebrities of sport with the marketing of products, he created a global industry led by his own International Management Group (IMG) and, along the way, became one of the most admired and honoured entrepreneurs of his time. After Mark, nothing was ever the same again. I know; I was there at the beginning.

It is October 1960. Arnold Palmer is going to be *Sports Illustrated* Sportsman of the Year and I have been assigned to the story. Arnold and I are in the clubhouse after the opening round of the Sam Snead Invitational in Huntington, West Virginia. Arnold orders a hamburger. The waitress brings it with a bottle of Hunt's ketchup. Arnold looks up and says, 'Don't you have Heinz? Well, you should.' Turned out that the most famous golfer of his day – if not the most famous golfer ever – was being paid nine dollars and sixty-one cents a week to say he used Heinz ketchup.

Enter Mark McCormack, who had recently made his famous handshake deal to represent Arnold Palmer. The IMG files, as complete a corporate record as you could hope to find, records the correspondence between a frustrated McCormack and the poker-faced H. J. Heinz, which confirms that Palmer had indeed signed the sub-$10 contract which even included the glowing advertising language in which he could be quoted as a Heinz ketchup ambassador. That was the way things used to be before Mark. The sports business has come a long way since then.

Lots of things began to happen. As the 1960s went by, Mark often asked me for advice.

Could tennis ever be a big spectator sport? No way, I said. Too simple a game. So he signed Newcombe and Laver and Evert.

Should he get into skiing? No. Who cares about skiing? So he signed Jean-Claude Killy.

Should he expand worldwide? No way. Sport is too regional and weird. Soccer, cricket, badminton, snooker, for heaven's sake.

Tents at Wimbledon for sponsors and guests? Gross commercialisation. Anyway, they'll never let you do it.

I don't recall exactly when Mark stopped asking for my advice.

Instead, he would give me the latest IMG bulletins over dinner. The Royal and Ancient Golf Club (R&A) loves its tents. The Golf Annual is going to be published every year forever. We have artists – come and meet Kiri Te Kanawa at the Met. We're going to have the biggest model agency in the world. Know who's the largest independent producer and distributor of sports media? There was no end to it. Like liver? We bought Strasbourg's football club. Like tennis? We bought the ATP events at Indian Wells and Miami. Like reading? My *Harvard* book has sold more than a million copies. Like cricket? We partnered with cricket boards from India to the West Indies. We've signed the IOC, the ISU, the NFL, the USGA – a whole alphabet soup of sport would spill out across the table as the hors d'oeuvres and bread kept vanishing.

The names and the years flew by. Navratilova, Gretzky, Montana, Jeter, Woods, Mark always relishing the return of wanderers (Faldo is back; Sampras is back), generous in his support for those down on their luck, and outlining his designs on those who had not yet seen the light: the Pope, Margaret Thatcher, Bill Clinton, Jack Welch. They all needed IMG he said. He told them why, and most of them agreed.

As the dinners evolved from no-star Tex-Mex to two-star French, I began to get a glimmer of a very complex man. I came to understand that his goal was not fame. He did not want it. His goal was not money. Most of the profits of IMG were ploughed right back into IMG.

Mark's goal, his thing, was IMG itself, what it stood for and could accomplish, much of it in ways that nobody had ever thought of. He loved competing and he hated to lose. His unchanging goal in life was to make IMG a winner. His focus was legendary. The whole enterprise was based on synergy, the forging of an extraordinary network of mutually beneficial rather than competing interests.

This is the Mark that you'll find celebrated in so many ways in this book. He was a friend who never forgot you, a friend always looking for the next, new thing, an astounding visionary and an entrepreneurial genius. The wisdom in these pages is testament to the fact that we still have lessons to learn from him.

Ray Cave
Former editor, *Sports Illustrated* and *Time* magazine

street smart [def.]

An applied people sense... the ability to make active, positive use of your instincts, insights and perceptions

Mark H. McCormack,
What They Don't Teach You at Harvard Business School

Introduction

Ours was a relationship based on mutual respect, admiration and trust. We considered each other's word to be his bond when we first established our business association ... A handshake, nothing more, was the cement that bonded us.

Arnold Palmer

It seems hard to believe that the modern sports business started with a handshake, but that's exactly what happened when, back in 1960, the world's number one golfer, Arnold Palmer, agreed to be Mark McCormack's first big client. It turned out to be a handshake that would change the sporting world forever.

McCormack's great idea was a deceptively simple one: he believed that the best athletes had a commercial value that was not being realised, and that there was a business to be built in helping athletes to maximise that potential. Why shouldn't he represent sporting talent, just as he represented clients in his legal practice? He also had the experience to know that to get the idea off the ground, he needed a rising star and, as a golfer himself, he recognised in Arnold Palmer the perfect partner.

That apocryphal handshake was the start of what would become McCormack's International Management Group (IMG), a global business that created an entirely new industry where professionally represented sportsmen and women competed in an ever-expanding series of showcase events around the world, beamed into the homes of merchandise-hungry sports fans via television. The world really would never be the same again.

Broadcaster Alistair Cooke made McCormack the subject of one of his *Letters from America*. For Cooke, McCormack's influence was unequivocal:

> *McCormack was the Oracle. ... [He was] the creator of the talent industry, the maker of people famous in their profession famous to the rest of the world, making them a fortune in the process ... He took on as clients people already famous in their profession as a golfer, opera singer, author, footballer, racing car driver, violinist – and from time to time, if they needed special help, a prime minister, or even the Pope.*

As IMG grew and expanded, so did McCormack's reputation as a businessman and entrepreneur. Not surprisingly, people wanted to know what he had to say. Enter Mark H. McCormack the best-selling author. When *What They Don't Teach You at Harvard Business School* was first published back in 1984, it became an instant bestseller, spending 21 weeks at number one on the *New York Times* bestseller list and selling over a million copies worldwide.

The author himself was characteristically straightforward about the book: 'I wrote *What They Don't Teach You at Harvard Business School* not to take swipes at a great business school or to brag about my triumphs in 25 years of corporate warfare. Frankly, the book was born because I wanted to write down ideas I had been thinking out loud for years in the course of doing business.' His aim was not to write the definitive guide to doing business, but to share his own thinking about being a 'street smart' executive, defined as the ability to use instinct, insight and perception to read people and business situations and act accordingly. So was born the idea of the 'street smart', a nugget of business information that uses an anecdote to bring to life a lesson from the real world of business. Out of the original book came a number of sequels and even a *Success Secrets* newsletter.

The fact that *What They Don't Teach You ...* is still in print today is testament not just to McCormack's vision but also to the enduring appeal of his business strategies and tactics, and the no-nonsense way in which he was able to communicate his ideas.

McCormack died in 2003, but his legacy and business philosophy live on. In the preface to the original *Harvard* book, he wrote, 'In fairness to Harvard Business School, what they don't teach you is what they can't teach you ...' This new book has been written with this philosophy in mind. It celebrates McCormack's genius by bringing together a collection of new street smarts based on interviews with the people who knew, worked with and were influenced by him – colleagues, clients and competitors alike from the famous McCormack network of friends. The result is an affectionate tribute to the original *Harvard* book, featuring a stellar line-up of contributors from the sporting and business worlds, who show how a brush with McCormack could change the way you do business forever.

The book also offers an insight into why it was that Mark McCormack was able not just to build a global business, but also to have such a revolutionary and lasting influence on the sports industry throughout the world.

Jay Lafave, a former legal associate of McCormack and the first person McCormack hired to help him grow IMG, has thought long and hard about the why, and no one is better placed to provide an answer. His words speak volumes.

Why was Mark able to go so far and do so well? I don't think there is a single answer to that question, but there are a number of things that I think equipped Mark to achieve the success for which he is recognised:

1. *Mark was intelligent. He was well rounded with broad interests and was well received and comfortable in almost any social group.*

2. *Mark was perceptive. That's a little different from being*

just intelligent. He noticed and absorbed things better than most.

3. *Mark had a prodigious capacity for work – a great deal of it. He pushed himself to work harder than, or at least as hard as, anyone else, starting long before dawn and on and on, well into the night and after dinner either in the office or on the road.*

4. *Mark was extremely well organised so that the work he did was by and large done very efficiently. The famous 3 × 5 index cards he carried in a jacket pocket consisted of a card or two for each member of staff, each client and each person with whom he was then transacting business. These notes were also recopied onto the famous yellow pad to create 'live' lists that he revisited and updated regularly. As part of that process, Mark would stop and think about every topic going on with every staff member, every client and every business option, which kept everything well organised and correct in his own mind.*

5. *He was punctual. Mark was always on time, which for him meant being present and ready to start a few minutes before any scheduled starting time. This was especially evident in Mark's phone commitments. If he told you he would phone you around 8.15 a.m. a few weeks or even months ahead, you'd better set your watch, because Mark would call you at exactly that moment from wherever he might be.*

6. *He set high standards for himself and for others around him. He wanted the best, to do the best, to be the best and to get the best. Mark set his goals with the best always just beyond his comfortable reach.*

7. *Mark was focused on profit; for him it was a dominating obsession.*

8. *Mark was a forward thinker, focusing always on the future.*

9. *From the very beginning, he was thinking internationally. Early clients included Gary Player, a South African golfer who had already won the Open Championship, and Bob Charles, a New Zealander. Mark also believed that to be a great golfer a client must win major events all over the world and against the best in the world, wherever they might be. That international viewpoint shaped Mark's thinking about the business he was developing. We thought of it as one world.*

10. *Mark had a way of inspiring those who worked for and with him, and as such was a successful leader of people. It seemed to me that people who worked with or for Mark each felt they had a kind of inside track with him. They became very loyal supporters of Mark and later of IMG. While Mark was clearly the leader, he had a way of making everyone feel really important.*

These are the qualities that combined to put Mark just a little ahead of his peers. When we were beginning back in the 1960s, people used to talk about finding 'a million dollar idea'. Well, there weren't that many who could actually get a million dollars from a million dollar idea – but Mark was one that could.

You'll see these 'qualities' illustrated in this book again and again, whether from McCormack's senior IMG colleagues, more junior staff who benefitted from IMG's enabling culture, the talent IMG represents, or a generation of contributors who never knew McCormack personally, but are influenced even today by his legacy, including graduates from the Department of Sport Management at the University of Massachusetts that now bears his name.

As with the original *Harvard* book, the contributions have been organised into three thematic parts, focusing on the key street-smart areas of 'People and relationships', 'Negotiation' and

'Growing a business'. Each part includes a series of anecdotes and lessons designed to build a picture of the McCormack way of doing business.

But perhaps the final word should go to Arnold Palmer:

I never had a moment's regret that I placed so much of my future in Mark's hands. It proved to be the right thing for both of us, and we attained success beyond our wildest dreams.

We hope that what follows will give you some pointers to business success too.

PART 1

People and relationships

1

Building relationships

Business situations always come down to people situations.

It's no accident that the opening part of *What They Don't Teach You at Harvard Business School* is devoted to **people**. Mark McCormack (MHM) firmly believed that understanding people and their motivations and using that understanding to build long-lasting relationships is the basis of business success. This may sound simple. It's not. It requires skill, dedication and a good deal of street smartness.

Mirroring the original *Harvard* book, *Beyond Harvard* also opens with a focus on 'People and relationships'. The chapters that follow are full of examples and tips for how to build and nurture relationships – with colleagues, clients and suppliers alike – while developing and using the people skills that are the very essence of being a street-smart executive.

When president of the World Bank Jim Kim first encountered MHM's advice he was, perhaps ironically, studying at Harvard. For him, a down-to-earth focus on people and getting things done made a refreshing change from a day-to-day diet of data and academic argument from those he describes as 'seminar-room warriors'. What he learned then about building deep relationships with people, finding great talent and supporting it, has stayed with him throughout his career. He provides an eloquent opening for our first chapter on 'Building relationships', and anticipates many of the themes that follow.

Good personal relationships can only oil the wheels of any business relationship. You don't need to be best friends with everyone, but showing an interest in people as people and spending time with them outside formal business settings will prove invaluable. **People really do like doing business with people they like.** MHM was a master at using informal and social events to build business bridges and make contacts, most obviously perhaps in the IMG hospitality marquees at places like Wimbledon or the Chelsea Flower Show, but also sometimes in the most unlikely places, as his friend and business associate, David Gilmour, reminds us. According to Bob Latham, MHM was 'linked in before there was LinkedIn'. People enjoy connectors and connections and it's always worth making efforts to bring people together and be open and generous with your networks.

Never underestimate, though, the time it takes to get to know people and understand what makes them tick, what motivates them. This is the famous MHM skill of 'reading' people. Listen and observe, he advised; be aware of your own strengths and weaknesses; develop insight – all advice on show here from his colleagues and business associates. Be able to empathise. **Empathy leads to trust, which underpins all business relationships**. Former IMG executive, Julian Brand, tells us about the importance of empathy in building IMG's relationship with World Rugby; Ian Todd and Howard Katz show how empathy and understanding make for the very best internal relationships too.

Investing time in *maintaining* relationships can also be crucial to doing business down the line. **Building and maintaining relationships is often a long game.** Robert Kraft, owner of the NFL's New England Patriots, got to know MHM over many years, although they did not do business together for the first twenty or so. But when the time came, the trust and understanding between them resulted in a deal conducted in just one short phone call. Invest time in relationships and stay in touch even if there's no immediate business reason to do so. Golfer Jack Nicklaus reminds us that the fact that he and MHM always kept the door open to working together ultimately led to one of the most lucrative deals of his career.

Putting personal relationships at the centre of business strategy means that **you also have to work at creating the right impressions**. The way you behave – in MHM's words, 'the conscious and unconscious statements you make about yourself' – really matters. It's important to be consistent; to mean what you say; to be patient, generous and discreet. For ex-chief executive of The All England Lawn Tennis Club, Chris Gorringe, this kind of business integrity made it possible to develop the trust for the commercial development of the Wimbledon brand that would otherwise have been inconceivable. Similarly, sticking with people, especially during tough times (witness Monica Seles' story), creates another form of trust.

You also need to **be prepared for any sort of business interaction.** 'Taking the edge' by doing your research shows respect, improves your insight and helps you make connections. It also impresses. IMG's Guy Kinnings remembers MHM's ability to recall an extraordinary, and always striking, amount of detail in client meetings. It's these kinds of personal touches that so often make the difference that matters.

The stories that follow show the enormous impact MHM's capacity for relationship building had on colleagues and clients alike. Many have adopted his tips and techniques into their own business practice. Time, then, to learn from them too.

Relationships trump theory

The first time I encountered Mark's business advice, I was in the middle of my medical and graduate studies at Harvard and helping to run an NGO that focused on providing health care for some of the poorest people in the world. I was moving back and forth between some of the greatest hospitals in the world, to seminar rooms at Harvard, to desperately poor villages in Latin America. In the middle of that jarring contrast I found that Mark's insights were always helpful. Harvard was full of 'seminar room warriors' who would argue at great length about arcane points, believing that winning the argument, at times with prejudice, meant something beyond the classroom. The view, which I agree with, was that in academic settings, you had to be dogged and uncompromising in the pursuit of truth, and it was data and academic argument that was the coin of the realm. I don't think Mark would have dismissed those pursuits but over and over again he would say that success in life is all about relationships and how you make people feel. The Pulitzer prize-nominated Maya Angelou would say almost the same thing later: 'I've learned that people will forget what you said, people will forget what you did, but people will never forget how you made them feel.'

In talking with people who knew Mark and did business with him, it has become clear to me over the years that he understood human beings in a profound way and, more importantly, he used that understanding to actually get things done. Mark helped me to see that achieving our highest aspirations for ending poverty, or providing treatment for HIV or other complex medical problems in the poorest settings, would not be possible if we didn't pay attention to issues like good management, good relationships with people who might have started out as our enemies, and a kind of discipline that was natural to a great businessman like Mark but less in evidence in many academic settings. So many of the things that are worth doing in life require getting groups of people to do things that they would otherwise not normally do, and I knew that Mark's advice would prove to be more helpful than just trying to win arguments or be the smartest person in the room.

Mark helped me to understand that the greatest achievements, the most extraordinary goals, require that leaders build deep relationships with people, find great talent and then support them to be successful. Of all the challenges I've ever tackled, leading and supporting others is both the most difficult and most rewarding of them all. With early inspiration from Mark, I've continued to work with a great coach, Marshall Goldsmith, and work on becoming a better leader every single day.

Jim Kim

Connections can be made even in the most unusual places

Around 1970, I used to stay at the Beverly Hills Hotel in California, which was known as the Pink Palace in those days. A favourite hang-out at the time was the Polo Lounge. I was there one evening when they had locked the door and the bar was closed. The only people left were clients who just wanted to stay for a nightcap. There were three banquettes together placed like ducks in a row. I was in the middle. To my left was Frank Sinatra and to the right someone I didn't know.

As we were supping our drinks, the side door from the kitchen was suddenly flung open and in burst a photographer, carrying a huge camera with big flash bulbs. He rushed straight over to Frank, who was sitting there with a woman, and shoved the camera in his face. Without hesitation, Frank got to his feet, picked up the ashtray from the table, whacked the photographer across the face, and knocked him out cold. It all happened right in front of me. I looked down and there was the photographer lying unconscious at my feet. Meanwhile Frank sat back down, lit another cigarette, and calmly carried on smoking and talking to his companion.

I was a bit shaken by the whole incident and I turned to my right to see this person staring at me from the other banquette. It was Mark. We looked at each other and shrugged. I got up and picked up the photographer by the feet, Mark picked him up under his shoulders and we carried him back out to the kitchen, and had the staff call the equivalent of 911. We never heard a thing about it in the press or anywhere. After that, Mark and I just started to chat. After an hour we realised we had mutual interests, so we arranged to meet for breakfast the next morning and that was the start of a lifelong friendship and business relationship. You never can tell where and when you'll make a connection.

David Gilmour

Keep the door open

I first talked to Mark from a business standpoint late in 1961 when I was about to turn professional. I had enjoyed success as an amateur but was driven by the belief that to be the best I needed to beat the best, which meant testing my game at the professional level. At the same time, I wanted to know what might be available to me if I decided to turn pro. Mark was in the business when no one else really was and was already working with Arnold Palmer and Gary Player, so I went with him. I stayed with Mark until 1970, by which stage I had won quite a few tournaments, including seven professional majors. Although there were no world golf rankings at that time I was probably considered the number one golfer in the world, and consequently, I felt that I could be doing better financially. Understandably, Mark's first priority was to Arnold and then Gary, and by that time he had also signed up other athletes, so it seemed to me he was spread very thinly. Being a pioneer means that there will inevitably be growing pains and learning experiences. I thought he needed to open up and bring some additional talented and smart people into his business.

Over the course of the next twenty-five years, I kept a good relationship with Mark. I liked him, and while we were not linked professionally, we enjoyed a nice personal relationship. We saw each other quite often and would sit down and talk. When I left to start my own company and manage my own business, it wasn't adversarial. It was just that I thought I could do a better job for myself.

In the mid-1990s, I was winding down my competitive playing career and looking for someone who could handle my growing international brands and licences, and take them forward as a legacy for my family. We had been doing it ourselves up until then. I thought it was a good idea to go back to Mark and rehire IMG on a limited basis. He was absolutely delighted. Mark himself arranged a contract for me with The Royal Bank of Scotland, and it was probably the best contract I have ever had. I think he worked every aspect of the deal himself because he was disappointed with the way things had turned out the first time we partnered decades earlier. But, this time, he negotiated the deal, brought it to me and then turned it over to one of the very good people he now had working with him.

In the intervening years, we had all grown up a lot. Without saying it, I think Mark felt that he might not have done for me what he should have before, and that he would like to ensure that the RBS deal worked well, and it did. He did a really good job with it. The important thing was that we had maintained a good relationship, left a friendship in place, and the door open for future business.

Jack Nicklaus

Show empathy

There is an oft mistaken view that successful salesmen need to be smooth-talking extroverts who can cajole the customer into buying with a 'close, close, close' attitude to selling. I had formal sales training before I joined IMG and the theory of 'set up, answer objections, and close' was drilled into us.

What Mark excelled at was the relationship part of the sales process. Yes, the product must be relevant and the pricing fair and proportionate, but all things being equal, customers want to buy from someone they like and trust. An ability to show empathy and understanding of the client's objectives while also humanising the sales process with personality and humour will go a long way towards getting yourself 'liked'.

My relationship with the International Rugby Board (IRB), the governing body of the sport of rugby (now World Rugby) showed just how important empathy and understanding can be. In 1991 the IRB appointed IMG to be its international sports marketing representative and sell all of its sponsorship and TV rights for the quadrennial Rugby World Cup tournament. The original deal was for one tournament only. We were set some aggressive sales targets but felt confident that we would achieve them. The greater fear was what would happen after the initial four-year period, especially as the US-based IMG, with very little knowledge of the sport, might not be seen as the most natural fit to market rugby's flagship event into the future.

It was clear to us from an early stage that simply raising revenues would not be enough. We set to work on really understanding their business and their issues, and proactively and frequently without instruction suggesting ways in which they could improve their offering. It wasn't all about the money – the IRB wanted the game exposed to as wide an audience as possible.

The proof of the pudding is in the eating, and IMG still represents World Rugby for the marketing of the Rugby World Cup. While our sales achievements helped build the Rugby World Cup into one of the world's largest sports events, I am convinced that the primary reason the relationship continues to thrive is because of the time we spent understanding and executing what World Rugby really wanted to achieve, and the strong personal relationships forged between executives on both sides.

In overseeing various sales departments at IMG I have always tried to ensure that my teams adhere to this principle. When I became involved in IMG's internship programme, I always signed off my presentations to the interns (all wannabee sports marketers) with the axiom: 'People do business with people they like to do business with.' It's a lesson I've taken with me throughout my business and personal life.

Julian Brand

Be generous with your networks

I have had the good fortune to work for several outstanding chairmen, including both Kerry Packer and then Mark. Kerry and Mark were close friends and business associates. It was a strong relationship that had built up over time. Kerry provided financial support in the 1970s, which saw Mark out of a difficult situation, and the support was reciprocal.

The two had markedly different approaches to networking and relationships. Kerry was very selective in the associates he dealt with around the world. He didn't go seeking future business or personal opportunities whereas Mark was universal in his approach. He must have worked at it 24 hours a day, but out of it came a vast network that was of value both to him and those within it.

Mark was also very generous in the way that he opened up his network. At one point, Mark introduced Kerry to Jack Kramer, who had been a world number one tennis player and went on to become one of the most important people in the establishment of professional tennis. At the time, Kerry was deep in thought about setting up World Series Cricket, a rival to the established order of Test cricket, and Jack taught us a lot about how to develop a professional sport from an amateur sport. That was a very important aspect of Mark's relationship with Kerry, his ability to introduce him to people who would give him advice; in this case it helped lead to the construction of World Series Cricket.

We were able, through Mark, to form personal relationships with the chairmen and presidents of the organisations responsible for selling television rights, which cemented our long-term relationship with them. Mark wasn't selfish in that regard, and didn't keep contacts to himself. He was happy for us to have our own relationship with them. If they came to Australia we would entertain them, and similarly, if we were in the US or UK, we would meet them at events such as Wimbledon. He had the ability to keep everyone together but at the same time be the representative for both. We always dealt through Mark at the end of the day but a personal relationship with the heads of the organisations was also very good for us. It meant that if there was ever a line-ball decision as to who would get the rights if a competitor came in, it would more likely go our way.

Mark was a totally different personality to Kerry, so I observed how he behaved. I noted the communication that he maintained both with staff and clients, and saw what a strength it was in terms of building relationships and maintaining the business. It was the biggest lesson I learned, and something I have tried to emulate myself.

Lynton Taylor

Pace yourself

Mark was an extremely quick decision maker. If he had something on his mind he wanted to clear it up quickly, and be able to move on to the next thing. If he needed information or a report, he didn't like to wait. He surrounded himself with people who operated in the same way and understood his need to act fast. All the senior managers I met at IMG were unbelievably straight to the point. It was almost as if it was in their DNA to fit with the company's culture.

In Mark's world, business moved at a fast pace so that opportunities were not lost. However, that was not our world. In the watch business, new designs or technical improvements to products all take time and cannot be rushed. Mark was aware of this and would ask for my advice, particularly when his great friend and then Rolex chairman André Heiniger passed on the business to his son Patrick, who Mark did not know so well. He would ask whether now was the right time to put a suggestion forward, or should he wait a month?

My advice to him, which I gave in a personal capacity, as I could not be involved in business dealings between both companies, was always to slow down when dealing with Rolex. Don't upset anybody by putting them under pressure. Mark would always listen, knowing it was better to wait and meet with a more receptive audience than to annoy people by trying to force something through, even though forcing the pace might have been more in line with the usual way he did business. He knew and understood that, sometimes, the pace has to be dictated by the people you're dealing with, even if that's out of kilter with the way you usually operate.

Bertrand Gros

Take the time it needs

It's a great skill to be able to adapt your personality and expectations to suit your audience. For my second meeting with Mark, he told me to meet him at six minutes past nine and we would ride down in the elevator together. The ride in the elevator for thirteen floors and then the walk to his car would mean we had a minute and a half to talk about whatever it was he wanted to talk about.

Our meetings with Wimbledon, by contrast, would last a day. Mark could happily talk for two hours about whether a button on a shirt had been sewn on correctly when he knew that was important to the clients. He would take enough time to demonstrate that if he cared about something so small, imagine what he was doing with the big things. Allowing your audience to feel very comfortable and appreciate that you are going at their speed without imposing your will is both charming and disarming. It is yet another reason that relationships such as that between IMG and Wimbledon endured.

Ian Todd

Everyone is equally important

I was represented by IMG from the start of my tennis career, but I left for a year when I was around seventeen. IMG suddenly took on a lot of players, and my parents felt that I wasn't getting enough personal attention. We were sold a package by an alternative agency about me being the only female in the group, and how that meant they could devote more time and effort to me. There was discussion back and forth and it was a big decision to leave IMG. However, I decided not to bother Mark with what to him must be a small thing. I thought he really wouldn't care.

Afterwards he said, 'Why didn't you come to me?' I explained that I thought he had bigger things to deal with. He was upset that I had thought that, and said that he cared about everyone. He said he would have resolved any issues and could have switched me to having my own agent. But I just needed to communicate.

I was amazed that he was so concerned. It showed me what kind of person he was. He was at the top of an organisation involved in so many different areas, but he saw and cared about everything. I was young and it had been more my parents' decision to leave, but after talking to Mark I said to my mum and dad that we should think about returning. I was gone for less than a year and Mark was totally the reason I came back. I knew that if I ever needed anything I could go straight to him. I trusted him completely. I wasn't one of the biggest stars in the company, but I always felt included.

Mary Joe Fernandez

The power of emotional intelligence

According to the Center for Creative Leadership, 75 per cent of business leaders fail due to their lack of emotional intelligence. The higher up you go, the more at risk you are. Mark called emotional intelligence being 'people smart'. His approach was: use your insight, listen, and observe in order to read people and ultimately achieve your objectives. The more you understand the person you are dealing with in the context of their environment and situation, the more likely you are to achieve your objectives.

Ultimately, good work alone won't bring success without emotional intelligence. From personal experience, I never wanted to play the game, or deal with politics or acknowledge that I was a woman dealing in a man's world. I just thought I would work hard, deliver results, and achieve promotion on that basis. Then I got promoted to director level and realised that I had to learn to play the game. When you get to VP and C-Suite level it is even more important. You have to develop an ability to navigate what it is that you need, the company needs, your colleagues need, and what your boss and the board need. There are multiple stakeholders who will contribute to your success and you need to develop insight and emotional intelligence to create the right kind of strategies to be successful.

The word 'politics' often has a negative connotation. But if you look at it through the lens of 'good communication and emotional intelligence that will help you win the game and succeed', it starts to sound very positive. Mark made reference to the fact that people who complain about office politics or don't want to invest in themselves and play the game invariably become victims. I tell people my success is 100 per cent dependent on me. There are lots of people around me who can help me. I need good people around me who can help me be successful, but if I succeed I will know it is because I navigated it, and if I fail, it's because I messed up. You need to own your success and failure.

Stacey Allaster

Understand people's motivations

Not long after I joined IMG, Mark asked me to meet him for breakfast. He had heard good things about me but we really didn't know each other, so it was an interesting meeting. During the course of the breakfast, one of the things he asked me was what my career and financial goals were. I was only 24 or so at the time, so I had never thought about it. But he pinned me down, asking how much money I thought I wanted to be making by the time I was 30. His reasons were twofold. He wanted to make me think about financial and other objectives at specific stages of my career, but also to check that he was going to be able to help me realise those objectives. It was important that I had goals and that he could make sure they were achievable at IMG. If he hoped or thought that I was going to be working for him some day as a senior executive, he wanted to leave nothing to chance. Encouraging that sort of proactive thinking was very smart and planting the idea that he wanted me to grow left a deep impression on me.

When I did leave IMG nearly ten years later, he was respectful of my desires to broaden the scope of what I was doing, but we had a number of conversations about it. He wanted to understand why I felt I couldn't accomplish all that I wanted with IMG. It was important to him to understand why I had to leave in order to fulfil a career objective, primarily to avoid the situation arising again. He hadn't been able to control it this time, but would hopefully do so in the future. He also asked me to make a thorough report on the state of the company and my observations. I spent a lot of time writing it as I certainly owed him that. Both at the beginning and the end of my career at IMG, Mark took the time to find out about my motivations and to help me think about what was important to me and why.

Howard Katz

Know how people tick

Situations can be turned on their head if you know how to read people.

For one reason or another there was a point when I was thinking of leaving IMG with a couple of others, and taking Bjorn Borg, who I had signed and represented, with me. Mark got wind of the plan and suggested that we have breakfast together. When we met, he was amazingly relaxed and perhaps in a way admired the fact that we wanted to do our own thing. We had an extremely friendly conversation, and by the end of it he had won me round. He had an incredible ability to know which buttons to push to make people feel special. He said, 'I have cancelled everything else today. I'll spend as long as I need to get this resolved.' Straight off that made me think that I was important to him and to the organisation, knowing how Mark managed time.

He then went on to say, 'I want to resolve this, and if I do, I promise that I will never mention it again.' It was very clever of him to know that that would appeal to me. My heart wasn't totally in setting up a new venture, and Mark's comments helped sway me. His ability to handle that situation and his understanding of me and what was important to me, meant that I didn't go off and do my own thing and in fact stayed at IMG for another twenty-odd years. We resolved our differences and he was true to his word. He never once referred to my plan to leave, not even sarcastically or when he was mad with me, for the rest of my time there.

Ian Todd

Saving face

When it came to business meetings, Mark would say that, where possible, it is better to meet one-on-one, rather than have group meetings. It may be necessary to have group briefings, but often the decisions should be made or contracts agreed in individual meetings. This is in large part due to the concept of 'saving face'. Powerful people don't like losing face in front of subordinates. If two people can agree something in private, even if it has meant having to cede ground in a deal, neither party loses face outside the room. You can both come out and say, 'We have agreed'. For years, Mark closed deals on our behalf with just the head of sport at the BBC, and it is a practice I have followed.

The notion of saving face is important in many business contexts, but it is critical in certain cultural contexts. Dubai was hit very badly by the 2009 recession and was facing serious challenges. We had a cast-iron contract for a Tour event to be hosted in the region, but it was starting to look as if it would be impossible financially. The advice from a lot of people was to leave it to the lawyers to sort out. However, I could see that to involve third parties would be disastrous. Instead, it would be far better for the two sides to come to an agreement behind closed doors, without anyone having to lose face. We continued on our own without resorting to lawyers. Concessions were made, but they were nothing compared to what we would have spent in legal fees and the damage that involving others would have caused to our relationship. Happily, the event went ahead, our relationship continues to strengthen, and the DP World Tour Championship, Dubai, is a regular fixture in the Tour calendar.

George O' Grady

Do your research

Mark took a huge interest in the clients and would always ring up to ask how things were going with them. Even when I was very junior, I would have my twenty-minute slot with him whenever he was in London, and we would talk about the clients. When I signed a player I always used to say that we should go and have a cup of tea with Mark. They were, of course, signing with a big global company, but IMG was also very much about the inspiration, and the leadership of its founder. I would explain that Mark was a visionary who, among many other things, created the World Match Play, and the World Rankings. It wouldn't do any harm to meet him. For a lot it made sense, but for some youngsters the attitude was more like, 'Do we need to, what will we talk about?' I would tell them that, in my experience, twenty minutes with Mark and he would normally come up with something pretty interesting. It certainly wouldn't be platitudes.

I once signed a client who Mark had tracked for months. I phoned him to tell him and his response was, 'Brilliant, I want to meet him.' When they met, Mark told him that he could remember when he won the Guatemalan Amateur, and that that was when he really first noticed him as a player. The client was completely taken aback that Mark would have that much knowledge about him. It was a total surprise and I could see he was impressed. He was immediately engaged and from there, we went on to have a really good conversation about the importance of being a global player. As ever, Mark's commitment to knowing his clients and doing his research had made an impact.

Guy Kinnings

Make sure you're prepared

For a relationship to get off the ground, you have to invest time in preparation. It is never time wasted. Mark's preparedness was legendary.

Before I go into a room, I have to prepare myself. To be genuinely interested in everyone you meet is a personality trait that very few people have naturally. Before I walk in, I try to put myself in the right frame of mind in order that I can be genuinely interested in everyone in the room, that I can be enthusiastic about what they are saying, be open, and listen actively, or aggressively, as Mark would say.

Before my most important meetings, I spend a huge amount of time in preparation thinking about my relationship with the people present. I try to understand what is at stake for them, what is important to them, what they are trying to accomplish and how we can help each other. A relationship will grow if the other party can see that you agree that their goals are important, and you are doing everything you can to help them accomplish them.

Before I meet someone, I think about what is important to them in order to get off on the right footing. For example, when I met Secretary-General Ban Ki-moon, I spoke to him in Korean. I addressed him in the politest form of the language, clearly acknowledging him as my elder and superior. On foreign trips we took together, I walked two steps behind him, and insisted that he lead the delegation. I said to him, in Korean, 'I will simply carry your bag for you.' He laughed and said of course not, we are going to be equal, but the effort I made to understand him and to speak to him in a way that would make sense culturally, allowed us to develop a very warm and, more importantly, a very productive relationship.

In every situation, whether it's a meeting with a head of state or the head of a village in rural Haiti, I try to make myself ask, what is at stake for this person and is there something I can do to help them accomplish great things? If you can find a compelling answer to that question, you can usually enlist them in helping with your agenda.

Jim Kim

SHORT SMART

Mark taught me to always do my research on names and people who will be at an event or function. Before I go to a dinner or a meeting, I have my assistant research who will be there and I make notes that I can glance at when I need to. If you can sit down somewhere and bring up one fact about someone, people find it impressive.

Linda Cooper

Stay true to yourself

After the 1968 Grenoble Winter Olympics [at which Jean-Claude won three gold medals] I had offers like you wouldn't believe. I had one from a Hollywood agent who offered me $2,000 per month for the rest of my life. That was an incredible sum back then, especially for a guy from the mountains like me. It was unheard of. But Mark did not do that, which I really liked. He made no financial promises. He was down to earth and just talked straight. I think I am a good judge of character and I could see that he was not playing a role of any sort. He wasn't trying to be a 'super' agent, or a friend, or a father figure who would take charge. He was being himself, Mark H. McCormack, and that was what I wanted. I signed with him because he was professional, he knew the business and he had a heart.

I spoke hardly any English then, and the friend who had first introduced us acted as translator for us during our discussions. It was a couple of years later that, by chance, I heard Mark speaking perfect French to someone else. I was amazed and asked him if he had been practising because of me. He explained that no, he had majored in French and had been able to speak it for years. He had just chosen not to. That was typical Mark and totally to his credit. He could have impressed me with his French when he first met me but he did not, because he didn't want that to be a distraction. He underplayed everything and focused on what was important: mutual respect and building our relationship.

Jean-Claude Killy

SHORT SMART

First impressions matter. When you meet someone, give them a firm handshake, a smile and look them in the eye. Particularly for women in business, these gestures signal confidence, authority and your interest in establishing a positive relationship.

Val Ackerman

Plan, organise, develop

When a relationship works well, it should feel completely natural. But, in reality, it takes vision, planning, organisation and development.

When Mark socialised, everything was recorded. If he played tennis with somebody, he would make a note of the score, and do so from one year to the next, in order that a handicap could be awarded, either to his opponent or himself. It was an immediate talking point, and prompted a shared interest. Arranging a game of tennis might look natural, but it was all incredibly organised and well thought-out.

There are different stages in building a relationship. The first stage is socialising, whether at a dinner out together, hospitality at Wimbledon, a game of golf, or perhaps a ProAm tournament. From there you might find a small angle, a means of becoming more intimate. I was once at an event with an influential banker whose wife was fanatical about Nadal. I followed up by having his tennis shirt signed and delivered to her. The relationship was catapulted to the next level overnight.

The second stage is improving an existing relationship. We represent the Giro d'Italia World Tour cycling event, one of the most beautiful and challenging races in the world. Each year we invite a special group of clients to cycle two or three stages of the race ahead of the professional riders. Everything is organised to the highest degree, but the real benefit comes from each individual pushing themselves to their physical and mental limits and the spirit of camaraderie that is fostered between riders as a result. It creates a unique bond, and relationships turn to friendships that go way beyond a business interaction.

It also means that you take care of that person if they slip or fail. You demonstrate your sincerity and that they are still your friend and you are not an opportunist. You keep inviting them to Wimbledon, and to parties where you can introduce them to people that will be helpful. You do it because you are a friend, but when they bounce back, they will remember that even more.

Michel Masquelier

Collaborate

Soon after I was named president of Turner Sports, we set out to expand our sports properties. We quickly learned that Wimbledon was going to become available after being tied up for many years with NBC and HBO. Since HBO was a corporate sister in Time-Warner, Seth Abraham – then president of HBO Sports – called to let me know that HBO was bowing out of negotiations, although NBC would probably stay in the game. I jumped at the offer when Seth volunteered an introduction to Mark McCormack, about whom I had heard so much. A joint meeting was arranged with Mark, NBC and Turner.

I soon found myself on a couch in Dick Ebersol's office, trading pleasantries with Mark, Dick and Ken Schanzer. We explored the possibility of a three-way deal among NBC, Turner and The All England Lawn Tennis Club (AELTC).

I won't forget Mark's opening remark to me, which immediately reflected the value he placed on creative interaction. 'If we work together,' he said, 'this can have a good outcome *for all of us.*' His comment had great resonance for me – and through my dealings with him over the years to come, that sense of relationships and the building of trust grew through every phone call, meeting, meal and social occasion.

Mark's collaborative approach did not simply help forge strong relationships with the people in the room. He was at the same time creating value for his client. He was able to put people together and construct a deal behind the scenes, work through all the differing elements and package it perfectly for the AELTC. What came out of the other side for the client was a wonderful meal – without the need for them to see any preparation in the kitchen.

After our successful launch of Wimbledon, I mentioned to Mark the company's desire to expand more into golf. I knew IMG represented the Royal and Ancient Golf Club (R&A) and that their deal for cable rights would soon be up for grabs. Mark and I met with Peter Dawson, chief executive of the R&A, and again Mark brokered a deal built on trust and common interest that forged new relationships and kept all parties happy. His work then and subsequently in fostering that relationship helped make it possible for the Open Championship and its other events to come to NBC, which has been my corporate home since 2011. The best collaboration is always in the interests of all parties in a negotiation, and taking the time to build trust and relationships naturally leads to other business opportunities.

Mark Lazarus

Bring people together

When corporate hospitality was first introduced at Wimbledon, Mark called me up and explained the concept, asking if I would sign up. I immediately agreed to take one of the first six marquees. It was one of the best forms of customer engagement we ever did, and one that we continued for many years.

The benefit of corporate hospitality is that it creates an environment where two people can talk to each other and discover whether they have a mutuality of interest. It moves the relationship beyond a business transaction. From that may come a creative idea and things move forward. Much of business is built on relationships, and in building relationships, you cannot be prescriptive. A relaxed environment allows matters to develop at their own pace.

Mark fully understood the importance of relationships and network building, and it was something I benefitted from. As just one example, it was through him that I met Ben Bidwell, then general manager at Ford Motor Company. Mark was running a golf event in Scotland for Rolex. I was invited to go up and meet all the people in Rolex and all the people who worked with Rolex, like Ford. One of the businesses I was involved with at the time was in the automotive sector. Through my initial round of golf with Ben, we developed a relationship with Ford which then led to my meeting Jacques Nasser, Ford's CEO and president. It helped cement our relationship in supplying components to Ford and enhanced our business.

Once he had put parties together, the business benefits could flow between the parties and back to IMG. Mark trusted that the parties he put together would have a mutuality of interest, would behave properly in respect of each other and would reflect well on IMG. That was a judgement he made with each of his relationships. His careful judgement of people and ability to build his network through bringing people together was something I experienced, learned from and developed over many years.

Sir Christopher Lewinton

Mix and match

Mark McCormack was linked in before there was LinkedIn. He was a connector before Malcolm Gladwell defined the term. He referred to these dynamics as an 'organisation system' – a way to keep track of people, time and issues. His was a system of note cards on which he would be constantly jotting so that he could instantly recall something or someone, and follow up in a timely fashion. I've used a similar system, albeit with more modern tools. My electronic notes (some might say a database) are organised by places, occupations and any number of other factors, although I don't know that it is any better than Mark's note cards. As I travel in my day job as a lawyer and in my positions in sports, I implement his lessons. If I'm in London on legal business and have a sliver of time, I'll try to connect with somebody from the rugby world. If I'm in Auckland for a rugby reason, I will try to connect with a legal or business colleague.

Along the same lines, he greatly enjoyed, and found instructive, mixing diverse groups of friends, clients and business associates. One time, by sheer coincidence, I was checking into The Four Seasons Hotel in Chicago at the same time he was. He had pre-organised a dinner but said, 'join us'. Having been part of his mix on multiple occasions, I saw its benefit (I remain in touch with a number of people who I met in a social setting with Mark), and always look for opportunities to do it myself. For instance, I spent a considerable amount of time at the Rugby World Cup when it was held in England. During that time, a number of my law partners from the US passed through London on business, as did a few clients. I brought them along to rugby events and functions and introduced them to some of the legends of the game. The standard reaction from each of them was: 'Now I know why you spend so much time doing this stuff!'

Don't be afraid to let your various lives meet. People enjoy connectors and connections. It can also deepen friendships and, as Mark said and proved, people prefer to do business with friends.

Bob Latham

Treat people as people

I was very young, just thirteen, when I first met Mark and his wife Betsy [Nagelsen]. I knew Betsy from the tour and had always liked her, and through her I met Mark. My parents soon saw that they were both quality characters, and that counted for more than anything else. At that stage everybody was doing everything to sign you and offering everything, but their approach to me, how they were as human beings and how they saw me, meant so much more. When Mark said something, you didn't need a piece of paper or twenty lawyers to look through it. He was a man of honour and that is very rare in our industry and in life. With the ideal partnership, you shake hands on something and both parties adhere to that agreement, both through the happy and the difficult times. The former is easy, but the latter tests those partnerships. I was thankful that both my parents saw the right qualities in Mark and, somewhere a little further along the way, I did too.

Although I had other IMG agents work with me, Mark took a personal interest and would call regularly. He would call up and say, 'Hey, I'm going to be in Paris. Are you going to be there too? Is everything good?' And always, he would ask, 'are you happy?' It wasn't just about my results.

Mark played a tremendous role in my comeback. [In 1993, Monica was stabbed mid-match in Hamburg, Germany by a fanatical Steffi Graf fan. At the time, aged nineteen, she was ranked world number one and had already won eight Grand Slams]. He and Betsy welcomed me into their home at a very difficult time and gave me unconditional support. They came to support me in Toronto at the Canadian Open, my first tournament over two years after Hamburg. They came to every single one of my matches for the whole week. A person operating at the level that Mark was, and with a schedule as hectic as his, they don't have to do that sort of stuff.

What I had to go through was a unique experience. No one else has ever had to face that situation, so there was no blueprint as to 'what to do with Monica'. I was a teenager, and number one in the world at that time. We had a meeting at Mark's home in Orlando and he said you have enough money never to play tennis again. Tennis is important to you, but whatever you choose to do, we just want you to be happy. The bottom line was seeing me as a human being, not just as a client that could raise a lot of money. That speaks volumes. To Mark, once he was your friend, he was your friend, and an incredibly loyal one. In my situation, he could have started to wonder where the revenue was coming from. That was never once an issue.

Monica Seles

Humour: the true test of friendship

People enjoy doing business with a friend rather than a stranger and especially if they are people who act with integrity and who can be trusted.

Mark built a very strong network of friends from business contacts, people to whom he was intensely loyal. There was one particular group called the Eekcuf, all chief executives of major companies, who would meet at a wonderful venue like Gleneagles, for drinks, dining, golf and a lot of fun. The outings were such a success that they soon became a 'tradition', an annual event that was firmly in the calendar. Early on, one of them said, 'Well, we had better have a name if this is to be a regular thing. We've all been doing business around you Mark and been screwed, which makes you the REKCUF [read backwards] and us the EEKCUFs!' They loved to tease Mark that all of his friends had been sold sponsorship packages to IMG events. They each had a good relationship with him and liked him, even though they knew he was looking to do business with them. Even midway through a joke, he would be thinking of the next business opportunity or angle. The friendship made that all the more likely to happen.

Mark always wanted us to adopt the same approach, to make friends in the industry and build our own traditions. He was appalled if you had received an invite to a golf tournament and you did not take a business contact, even if the company was not paying for it, and it was not a work-related event. If you said you were going to be playing golf, it would be, 'Oh, why not take the vice president of programming at ABC?'

He was very cross if he found out that you hadn't maximised an opportunity to build friendships or cultivate networks. You would get a steely stare, and that definitely was not a good day. He understood the value of making the most of any opportunity to develop personal and business relationships.

Alastair Johnston

SHORT SMART

Humour is a great way to communicate. When Ian Todd left IMG, Mark made a brilliant speech and pulled out a memo from 1973 when Ian first joined the company. It was a memo his then boss had sent to Mark saying, 'Ian Todd has asked two perfectly reasonable questions that I don't know the answer to. One is: how much is he going to get paid, and the second: where is he going to sit?'

Buzz Hornett

Follow the Arnold Palmer model

Whenever we enter a contract, no matter what the original length of term, we are thinking of renewal right from the outset and how to strengthen the relationship. That's our first rule of engagement. How can we help this company in return for what they are giving me? How can we work this relationship so that it benefits us both and becomes something that will endure?

'We' is a valid term, as my relationship with IMG and head of golf Guy Kinnings is just as important as those with external companies. It is very much a partnership, as Mark's was with Arnold Palmer. I am very close to Guy both on and off the course – he was best man at my wedding and I am godfather to his daughter. Arnold had a very close relationship with Mark and together they forged relationships with companies that were sustained over many years. When he passed away, aged 87, Arnold was still the fifth-highest earning golfer, years after having retired. That is amazing and a model for us all. Young players should take heed. Many of them live in the here and now, but I am still, after 30 years, building ideas as to how I can improve my position in the future. There are a number of companies that I have worked with for over fifteen years and I am quite proud of that.

We are constantly looking for opportunities off the course, and there is no reason why I can't still be making money for decades to come. That approach and belief all stems from Mark McCormack and Arnold Palmer and their understanding of the value of building strong relationships that will endure. They changed the world of sport and we are still learning their lessons in many ways. Their relationship model is the one we all look up to.

Colin Montgomerie

Through trust comes longevity

The IMG/Wimbledon relationship began in 1968 and endures to this day. Mark could see that the long-term value of our relationship would far outstrip any short-term commercial benefits.

Take commission rates. Mark was always referred to as the 30 per cent man. If you had an ashtray, he would say, 'I can sell that on the marketplace for £1 and I'll keep 30 per cent. You still have a good deal as you have 70 per cent.' While the Club paid a flat rate on merchandising and on fees from official suppliers, on television the commission structure became much more flexible as rights fees exceeded everyone's expectations. Rather than insisting that a flat commission rate be paid, Mark would say to our chairman, 'I'm happy for you to decide what you think is fair.'

That led to IMG receiving television commissions only on the increase from the amount set in the previous agreement. Mark accepted our chairman's verdict on what he felt was fair without any quibble or quarrel – despite the fact that the sum would have fallen below what he contractually might have been entitled to – because he knew that by trusting us we would continue to trust him and work with him in the future.

Mark took a similar negotiating stance near the start of our relationship, when he introduced Rolex. At the time, IMG were responsible solely for television, and the commission from a supplier agreement such as Rolex would have gone to another agent, Bagenal Harvey. However, Rolex were Mark's client and it was entirely down to his work that they became involved with Wimbledon. Mark could have accepted the full commission, but to get out of a logjam, he accepted a split with Bagenal. It was another short-term 'financial loss' that was clearly in the long-term best interests of the relationship.

Trust was very important to us and we wouldn't have wanted to be associated with anyone who had a reputation for dishonesty, obviously, but also packaging. We didn't mind our media and sponsorship rights being packaged and sold together by one agent but we didn't want an agent of ours packaging Wimbledon with other events that he owned or represented. It could have been in Mark's financial interest to do so, but we never had the slightest reason to suspect that was happening. There is no doubt that Mark's integrity and trust has infused the entire IMG team that continues to serve the Club over 40 years later.

Chris Gorringe

Business relationships are complicated

For 25 years, HBO and NBC shared US television coverage of Wimbledon. During that time, I built a strong relationship with the executives at The All England Lawn Tennis Club, for whom I felt genuine affection. There were clear dividing lines – on anything business-related I would deal with Mark, but every year HBO and the Club would have dinners together before the tournament that were purely social affairs. Twenty years into that relationship, the television contracts were once again up for renewal. For the first time, HBO and NBC had very serious competition, from Rupert Murdoch's Fox, who were pursuing Wimbledon very aggressively and made the kind of offer we couldn't possibly match. However, after further negotiations with Mark and the Club, Wimbledon made the decision to stay with NBC and HBO, leaving the extra Fox money on the table out of loyalty. It was an incredible gesture and exemplified the depth and power of the relationship between the parties.

Five years later, in 2000, it was again time to renew the contracts. I now had a new chairman at HBO who to my intense dismay had no interest in tennis and no intention of even negotiating for the Wimbledon contract. I tried everything I could to make him change his mind, but he stood firm. I decided that given my long relationship with the Club, I wanted to be the one to tell them. I did not want to go through Mark. I called Mark's office and worked out where he would be on a specific day and night, as I wanted to be able to reach him as soon as I had spoken to them. I then called the Club to arrange a meeting and flew over the next day to break the news in person. Straight after the meeting I went to my hotel room and rang Mark. I told him what I had done and all hell broke loose. He was absolutely livid that I had not acted through him as the agent of the Club. I explained that I had built up this relationship personally with chief executive Chris Gorringe and the Club and I felt that I didn't want the story filtered. I wanted them to hear from me that it wasn't my decision, that I had no choice, and that I thought it was wrong. But Mark didn't want to know. He hung up on me and we never spoke again.

For Mark it was a double betrayal. In his eyes, he had trusted that HBO would remember the loyalty that the Club had shown five years earlier. But more importantly, I think that when HBO, through me, built the relationship with the Club, he trusted that I wouldn't take advantage of that, and he felt I had betrayed that trust, with a client to whom he felt intensely loyal. The truth was that I never tried to short-circuit his relationship with the Club. I knew all the business went through Mark, and I thought he did a brilliant job representing the Club. But as in life, business relationships forged over 25 years bring their own complexities.

Seth Abraham

The value of professional service

When I won the US Open in 1968 there was a lot of media attention. An army of press reporters who were exclusively tennis writers followed you around, so tennis was well documented. However, from a marketing point of view, particularly in the UK, most of the opportunities were perceived as a bit low class and cheap. There was a definite feeling that you would be selling yourself and lowering your moral standards, and so there was trepidation about following that route and a desire for something better. Mark saw that and started using players in a more sophisticated way. Things started to change in the early 1970s, when you would start seeing a sportsperson in a smart commercial for a car rather than something tacky on the London

Underground. There was a level of excitement around IMG and I didn't consider signing with anyone else. It was a feather in your cap to be with them.

By the time I won Wimbledon in 1977 things had changed a lot. I was doing a lot of stuff but it was all beautifully discreet and elegant. IMG had a reputation as being more expensive to work with, but you knew that what was delivered would be good; you got your money's worth.

It was an all-encompassing service, which was fantastic. It wasn't just the commercial contracts. They looked after your taxes, banking, helped you with international affairs, whatever was needed. They would also help with investments, a number of which worked very well for me. Mark, Bjorn Borg and I once invested in a building on Marylebone High Street that was divided into apartments with a shop on the ground floor. It made total sense to me, as property was a good investment, and we sold pretty much at the top of the market. I wouldn't have done it had I had to do the whole thing on my own. I was also much more comfortable as Mark and IMG were prepared to back up their advice by investing their own money.

I was kept apprised of what they were going to do. You have to trust your financial people as they are the experts but I was always consulted, and asked for my opinion. I was interested enough to have a dialogue about each. I think they respected me because I kept abreast of things. But there's a big difference between being consulted and interfering. Problems happen when a sportsperson says 'I want to do this investment', and insists on doing it against the advice they have been given. I was told that we had done rather well as I hadn't interfered the whole time. But why would I, when the service I was getting was so professional?

Virginia Wade

When a phone call is enough

When we bought the New England Patriots in 1994, our first priority was to build a new stadium. In 1999 we broke ground on land we owned next to the old Sullivan Stadium, and privately financed what became Gillette Stadium. When the stadium was first announced, we did a deal with a local technology company for the naming rights. However, before the stadium had opened, that company had run into financial difficulties and we were looking to sell the rights to a new partner. We wanted a third party to help in the sales effort, and given the significant sums involved, there were plenty of companies knocking on our door offering large guarantees. However, I didn't talk to any of them. I just picked up the phone, called Mark and we were done in 30 seconds.

While Mark and I were close friends, we had never done business together before, so the call was not based on my prior experience of his ability to do a good job. Instead, it was testament to his having built a relationship and a foundation of trust and understanding with me over more than twenty years.

Mark lived by the ethos that business is about relationships, something I completely agree with. He lived his life touching people, building bonds, and sharing experiences so that he could make a phone call and accomplish something just because of the investment he had made in that relationship with somebody, although as it turned out, it was me that made the phone call to him.

I first met Mark in the 1970s, when he represented all the tennis players that mattered and I owned a team that was playing in World Team Tennis (the US professional league which had been founded by Billie Jean King). Over time we built up a strong and deep relationship, and would play tennis with our families, meet at football games and at Wimbledon, where he was like the sun with everything orbiting around him. I looked forward as much to meeting him and seeing his friends and spending time together as I did watching the tennis. Mark invested time in relationships with people he enjoyed spending time with, and maybe something would come of it for him, or maybe not. He loved helping friends, connecting people and creating opportunities that were good for everybody, and that was part of his allure. He was the greatest of all time at building relationships but I like to think intuitively that is how I live my business life as well.

Mark built IMG, which is, to this day, a global talent colossus. The foundation of it is still based on the strength of the relationships that Mark created individually. Now it is in the hands of my very good friends Ari Emanuel and Patrick Whitesell, and while no one will ever be Mark, I see a lot of Mark in them. I think that it is fitting and poetic that the legacy of a business built on relationships is now in the hands of people who treat the business in a similar fashion.

Robert Kraft

2

Motivating and engaging

In order to be effective, you have to develop lasting relationships inside the company as well as outside.

All of the principles of being people smart on show in chapter 1 apply in at least equal measure to the relationships you need to forge inside a company to get ahead. MHM set great store on recognising and supporting talent – and also on helping that talent figure out the best ways to get ahead while getting along with their peers. Chapter 2 showcases a range of these motivation and engagement strategies and techniques for both managers and managed.

IMG's Jan Felgate shows us how the attention MHM paid to external relationships was replicated in his internal relationships too, and how motivated it made her feel when he took the time to pop his head around her office door when he was in London or help out with client relationships: 'his accessibility was a boost to morale' – something Jean Cooke also remembers from MHM's visits to the Wimbledon Shop and back office staff every year.

As a manager, one of the most important things you can do is to instil confidence in people. **Be an enabler, boost self-esteem and look for talent in the widest possible pool**. You'll be rewarded. Linda Cooper makes the point that it's a great management skill to be able to push your staff but be there to help them along the way, something she benefitted from directly at IMG. It's also the best way of making the most of all the talent available to you.

MHM famously said that you should 'hire people who are smarter than you'. Look for smart, savvy people and have your eye on personal potential rather than too rigid a structure. Gavin Forbes and Michel Masquelier prove that recruitment can be an art as much as a science. Jeni Rose tells us that you sometimes need to hire in specialist expertise you don't already have. Jeremy Palmer-Tomkinson reminds us of the power of a collaborative culture. Reward performance, but **don't let formal job titles and silos get in the way of flexibility** and cross-functional working. Be as open and honest as it's possible to be. Transparency builds trust. Set a positive tone for others and don't be afraid of the three phrases that MHM lists as the hardest to say: 'I don't know; I need help; I was wrong.' As Ian Todd says, using them shows strength and confidence, not weakness.

Giving people the room to grow and make mistakes they can learn from is fundamental to personal satisfaction at work. Manage egos, but also support people when the chips are down. **Delegate effectively and as much as possible**. Peter McKelvey describes this as helping an employee feel comfortable about going out onto the thin part of the ice; and Alastair Johnston tells the fascinating story of how he gradually succeeded MHM as Arnold Palmer's key contact at IMG, a delegation crucial to the business as well as enabling for him personally.

Role models and mentors also **matter**. MHM described mentoring inside companies as a 'week-in, week-out, month-to-month proposition'. Michael Wright gives us a masterclass in how to deploy internal role models, while Bob Kain will never forget the lessons of practising with Billie Jean King at the top of her game. For him, learning from the best helped him to understand what being the best really means.

The ultimate test of whether internal relationships within companies are working is, of course, staff retention, mutual respect and loyalty. Tony Godsick has never forgotten the 'family feel' of IMG and has looked to replicate it in his own company. Read on to find out how MHM's tools for motivation and engagement can help you too.

Take an interest in staff

When I first joined IMG, my office in London was just down the corridor from Mark's. Whenever he walked past, which was about once a month, he would always stick his head around the door and have a chat about some of the latest tennis results or events. You needed to be on your game, as he could ask about matches that had been going on anywhere in the world in different time zones. But it struck me how valuable it made you feel as an employee when the chairman of the company, who had so many important balls in the air, took the time to engage with you directly, regardless of your level of seniority.

He was actively engaged in client activity during the US Open and often attended our IMG tennis division meetings at the French Open, and Wimbledon. Around 30 people would be present and the meetings could last up to five hours. Mark would stay for a significant portion of that time. Again, it amazed me that someone of his stature would come and listen to people discussing their problems – both small and large – and be actively engaged. He would take it all in and if he had something relevant to say, he would say it. He wouldn't problem-solve, but would offer to help where he could.

If we needed help recruiting a client, he was an asset. He would suggest making calls, or meeting the parents if we were trying to recruit a young player, or be on hand to assist when young players were training at the IMG Academy. He would open doors if you needed help getting into a brand. He was passionate about tennis and genuinely cared about what was going on, down to the smallest details. Once, following a meeting, I was asked to send around a list of our promising clients at the IMG Academy. I left off one up-and-coming, although somewhat obscure, Russian player and he promptly fired off an internal memo to me, asking me how I could possibly have forgotten her. Having him at the meetings proved his commitment and made us feel the support we had from him. His accessibility was a boost to morale.

It meant a lot to me to have him take an interest, both in formal and informal settings. I try, as a manager, to engage with my team regularly, as I know how much the personal touch matters. I try to make it easy for my staff to talk to me, and to ask for help. I'll try to initiate it too, saying come and talk to me, tell me what's going on, let's have a chat, tell me what's happening. Engagement is important at all levels.

Jan Felgate

Instil confidence

I have been associated with Mark's IMG for 30 years. That longevity is in large part due to the confidence that I have in them and that they have instilled in me, right from my first meeting.

When I was in my twenties and in my last year of study for a business degree, I had the opportunity to play a round of golf at Turnberry with two of Mark's closest work colleagues, Ian Todd and Peter German. While I knew I could play, I came from a conservative Scottish background, and professional golf was definitely not considered the way to go. I was very keen on the idea of working for IMG and I treated the round as a sort of job interview. Then I shot twenty-nine round the back nine holes, seven under par. At the last hole, Ian and Peter turned to me and said, 'Well Colin, you're not going to come and work for us, we are going to come and work for you!'

I couldn't wait to tell my father. His response was that if Mark McCormack's people think you can do it, then go for it. That was the kick and confidence boost I needed to get started.

Mark gave me confidence every time I met him. Fairly early

on in my playing career, I sat down for dinner with him and two others. I was amazed by the conversation. He was very interested in me as a person, my family and what made me tick off the course as well as on it. I was very taken by the fact that he was genuinely interested in what I had to say. There was no sense of 'what's in it for me?' And, given the stature of the guy, the fact that he had shown that interest made me walk away from that dinner with a huge amount of self-esteem and confidence, feeling that I belonged, that I was a part of the scene, and a part of what was going on. That feeling was reinforced every time I met him.

Mark's honesty, which was instilled in his staff, also inspired confidence. I have always been kept in the loop and not left in the dark, even when there is not particularly good news. Some deals fail or don't go well, not necessarily through any one person's fault, but it is always good to know about them. That transparency instils greater confidence than if things are kept from you. That's very important and a great asset within any business. With confidence comes trust, and with trust, the foundation of a sound and lasting relationship.

Colin Montgomerie

Honesty is the best policy

Being honest with a client will earn you more respect than trying to bluff your way through. If Mark had a meeting with clients and was asked six questions, only four of which he had the answer to, he would have no problem in saying so. He would say he would go and find the answer and come back to the client. They were often things that perhaps the client thought he ought to know, but that didn't stop him. The next time he spoke to that person, he would very clearly say: 'There were two things I couldn't answer the last time we met. Well, here are the answers now.'

He didn't feel he was belittling himself by saying that he didn't know. He saw it, rightly, as a strength, because the clients knew they could rely on what he said rather than some fudged answer. It gave them more confidence. It's very simple, but it's amazing how few people take that approach.

Ian Todd

SHORT SMART

Don't be afraid to ask for help. My dad was a brilliant businessman but if he didn't know something he was the first to put up his hand and say so. Asking others for help can flatter immensely and widen your circle of collaboration to great mutual benefit. Similarly, asking for help when you do know the answer can be extremely instructive as to who has their finger on the pulse of a situation.

Leslie McCormack Gathy

Let your people grow

One of the main reasons that senior people stayed so long at IMG was that they were given room to grow. Mark was an optimist and wanted to do everything. He wanted to build his legacy and make IMG a big global entity. He was always encouraging and open to suggestions. You never ran into a brick wall or a ceiling. You didn't need to leave or go elsewhere to grow, as you could always start something new within IMG, and know that you would be able to get on with it without being micro-managed. I did get offers from competitors, but I never really took those approaches seriously. I wanted to do a lot of things and not just manage a few people. When I started we were all agents. When I left, that was just 30 per cent of the business.

Because of this ability to grow, both as a company and as

individuals, I was able to hang onto some very talented people who might otherwise have left. I had a tennis agent who was doing a great job, who I switched into the broadcasting side of the business. However, he was definitely a character and found himself working under someone whose personality clashed with his own. It struck me for various reasons that he should try running IMG's modelling business, which at that time was floundering. He agreed to the move even though he knew nothing about modelling; he ended up being a superstar in this role, turning our modelling division from nothing into the number-one agency in the world. That felt great. Had we not been able to find other avenues, we would have lost a very talented person. Taking an open and creative approach to giving people opportunities and supporting them to grow will also lead to growth for the organisation.

Bob Kain

Every person counts

In a client-focused business, getting the smallest details right can be as important as the more headline-grabbing items. Mark was as interested in what merchandise we had in the Wimbledon Shop as in some great TV deal. And that certainly held true for the personal relationships he forged with the people he worked with.

IMG had meetings with The All England Lawn Tennis Club (AELTC) twice a year. The meetings were attended by everyone – from the people negotiating TV rights for significant sums down to me, who would be there to report on a £10k licensing agreement and the sales of T-shirts. Every detail was seen as an important part of the service we provided.

Part of the trick is to know what details to be involved with and what to leave well alone. Mark never interfered with day-to-day operations. He was interested and would say 'why don't you try this sort of product?' but that was as far as it went. Every Wimbledon Fortnight, he would come into the shop and ask what was new and what he should be looking out for, taking his time to choose Christmas presents. Where a lot of chairmen or CEOs would see that as a task to be delegated, Mark placed huge store by these sorts of small personal interactions. Of course, it also gave him the opportunity to gauge how the shop was operating so that he could talk with authority to the clients – another way he could demonstrate his personal interest and their importance to him.

This all came down to Mark's understanding of people, no matter what their position. During The Championships, he always took the trouble to visit the back office staff, who worked long hours without any of the glamour that people might attach to a major sporting event. It made their day.

And although it was common knowledge that he made notes of conversations he had had with you, it was still terribly impressive when your chairman remembered something you had said ages ago. My son was once taken ill and was in hospital, so I had to rush off at the end of Wimbledon. Mark rang me the next day to check how he was, which was very special. Getting the details right when dealing with people and making sure every person counts really does make a difference.

Jean Cooke

Be a talent spotter

When I first joined IMG, the company ran the many hospitality marquees at Wimbledon. Not long after I joined, the woman in charge left to go to Australia. Mark said, 'Oh, ask Linda to do it. She'll do a good job.' I was beside myself, thinking how on earth am I going to manage this? It was the first but not the last time that Mark would put me in situations that I really didn't think I would be able to cope with. I didn't think I could do it, but with Mark, there were no such words as 'no' or 'can't'. You just had to get on with it. All went well, as Mark knew it would, and that kick-started my career in all areas of hospitality creation and implementation.

I now do very much the same as I did at IMG but in a more niche business and have brought my hospitality experience to the high-end wedding-planning industry. I started when I saw that there was no one in the marketplace with my international experience and contacts. People wanted to get married in Paris, or New York, or Rome, and I had spent twenty years at IMG being thrown into cities and being told to just get on with it and build it. The confidence that that instilled in me allowed me to go on and establish my own business.

Mark saw ability in people. I don't know how many people in senior management positions actually look at their staff and see beyond what they are doing at the moment to what they might be capable of doing. You might have someone who is very well qualified but quite shy in business situations and won't push themselves forward, and it is up to senior management to take those people and nurture and encourage them. I didn't have a university education, but in the same way that he spotted talent in the sporting world, Mark spotted talent in his staff and nurtured it. He pushed people and you learned so much that way. It is a great management skill to be able to push your staff but be there to help them along the way. And it's also a surefire way of making the most of *all* the talent available to you.

Linda Cooper

Promote from within

My mantra during my time at IMG was always: if you are in the right place at the right time with the right look on your face, you can get given any job to do. The first port of call for senior executives looking to fill roles was to scan the people who were already there. That was certainly my experience, and one that I passed on. I had a secretarial role that included responsibility for the company's insurance. Following on from that, I was asked to do HR by someone who said: 'You have mastered the knack of telling people things they don't really want to know in a way that they can accept and still be cooperative. That equally applies to HR. You should get into it and see what you can make of it.'

There was no formal structure for it at all. Up to that point, the HR role in the UK had been low level, someone who sorted the secretaries out, although there were about 300 people in London at the time. I took on the role and made it my own. I didn't know anything about HR. But I knew the people, and I was trusted. If a new job came up developing a new aspect, it was all about your fit. Did you get it, were you intelligent, could you handle yourself, could you run with it if given the opportunity? If you understood the business, the pitfalls, how it fitted together and who to talk to, you could make it work.

Promoting from within works as long as you have good recruitment at the outset. We didn't want to recruit a 'career' anyone. We wanted to recruit people who could get in, understand the organisation, and be capable of going off in different directions. So many people in IMG started as lawyers. That put them in the spot of learning the business, seeing how contracts and deals were stitched together, how the company fitted together and delivered those services. After that on-the-job training, they were exactly the right person to become a client or event manager. They understood the fundamentals.

The mantra of 'right time, right place, right face' still applies. Take the world of TV production and digital media production. It has changed dramatically and clearly there will be times when there is a need for technical skills that you might not otherwise have. But still there is the drive to grow from within. Hire in smart, savvy people as runners or junior production assistants, and then let them grow into whatever role.

Caroline Ward

Repay loyalty with kindness

Generous acts from an employer will always spark reciprocal loyalty. In the sixties, Isao Aoki, a Japanese golfer and IMG client, had been playing a tournament at Gleneagles. As part of the tournament, there was a prize of a flat in the new development for anyone who holed in one. Aoki won it but couldn't have been less interested in the flat, so Mark bought it from him. He then offered it as a holiday house to any IMG employee who had been at the company for more than a year. You could book holidays for a week for up to six people on a first come, first served basis. It also included membership of the country club with free access to the golf courses, which was incredible. It was the same deal with his family property on Lake Michigan.

We were so well looked after in the event of accident, illness or general bad times, yet it was only in 1994 that we started taking on insurance or formalised policies for illness or bereavement. Until then, it came out of Mark's own pocket. The company always went above and beyond and there are countless examples of Mark's generosity to those who were struggling for whatever reason. That stayed in the culture throughout, that patience and acceptance that good people will sometimes have bad times. And those acts of kindness I have no doubt contributed to the long tenure of staff.

Caroline Ward

Family matters

Mark had been introduced to Tom Cruise through an executive at IMG who was married to Nicole Kidman's sister. He invited him to Wimbledon in order that he could get to know him better. He had also taken note, somewhere along the way, that my wife [former tennis pro Mary Joe Fernandez] was a big fan. Mark called me up and said: 'Tom's coming to Wimbledon and I know

Mary Joe loves him, so why don't you bring her over to the IMG marquee and we can have tea with him?' The tea, when it came, was a great success, with everyone getting on very well with each other. Tom was lovely and even invited us to the premiere of *Mission Impossible*.

Later that year, Mark called to say that Tom was in town and we should all have dinner together, but not to tell Mary Joe. It should be a surprise. Prior to the dinner I was sent detailed instructions, including a code word, 'mission', that I had to use to get to a private room in the restaurant. When we turned up, I whispered 'mission' knowingly to the hostess, who led me to a private room – full of my friends, there to celebrate my 30th birthday.

It turned out that Mary Joe had called Mark and said you are the only person who will be able to surprise him. He trusts you so much that he will be sure that whatever you tell him will be the truth.

I was impressed on many levels, but two thoughts struck me. Firstly, how creative he had been to conjure up an entire fake event. And secondly, how thoughtful he was to have taken the time to think the whole thing through given the mountain of other things he was dealing with. The fact that he cared left a deep impression on me.

Mark cared about everyone who worked for him, and created a family feel to IMG. At the smallest level, he remembered the names of people's wives and kids (or their favourite film stars), by writing them on his note cards and reminding himself at the right time.

On a bigger scale, by creating a family feel, he was able to keep his band of very talented, smart, hungry, aggressive, senior people together. He had different relationships with different people but he cared about them all. He created a culture where everyone wanted to win, but they were OK with winning as a team. Everybody worked together. He made everyone feel really important and was able to figure out how to keep everyone happy.

When I left to set up TEAM8, one of the reasons I chose the name was the play on words with teammate. My idea is to not only be teammates with my clients but with my employees. TEAM8 shows that it is important to me to incorporate that family feeling. I treat employees in my company a lot like Mark did, even keeping personal details about people in my iPhone, perhaps about their family or something that they're doing, or their favourite meal, so that when we meet again I can brief myself. I once said to Mark, I'm thinking of going to business school. He said why would you go to business school when I pay you to go to *my* business school? So I didn't go and he was right. There were many things I learned from Mark and the senior executives at IMG, and the importance of family was one of the biggest.

Tony Godsick

Boosting self-esteem

Whenever I went to the IMG offices I was always impressed by the people there. They were great. After I'd been a couple of times I noticed that every male had his name on the door of his office, but the female office managers, the receptionists and support staff – essentially all the people you meet when you first walk in – had no form of identification. Yet those people were the voice of the company. Every time someone called, or arrived at the office, they saw and heard the receptionists before anyone else – before any guy sitting behind an office door with his name on it. I asked them where their nameplates were and they initially dismissed the question saying that they did not have any. I persisted and said: 'Why not? Why don't you demand it? I'll ask for it if you want me to but I think you should learn to ask for what you want, if you want it.' And they all agreed it would be great to be recognised in the same way as the men, regardless of what their jobs were.

The next time I went in, they said, 'Billie, look!' and very proudly held up their name tags. It was such a minor thing but I noticed a big difference in their attitudes after that. It had created much better morale, and boosted self-confidence in the women. Now they had an identity, and were proud to be there, rather than just somebody sitting at a desk. And they had also learned an important lesson about asking for what they wanted and was important to them.

Billie Jean King

If the face fits, recruit

I first met Mark in Paris at the French Open. I was playing tennis on the circuit although I knew I wasn't going to do that well and wouldn't make a career out of it. Mark invited me to come and sit in his front-row box at Roland Garros, which to me at the time was a big deal. He had invited a number of other guests including my father Gordon, who had been a successful player in his time. One of the matches we watched was the Swedish player Mikael Pernfors in a quarter-final against Boris Becker. Mark declared that it would be a very quick match and that Becker would win quite easily. I had just finished college tennis and I knew that Pernfors was pretty good, especially on the slow red clay surface. I disagreed and said that I thought Pernfors would beat Becker. Mark loved to have bets and the stake was always a dollar. Sure enough, he bet me a dollar that Becker would win. I took the bet and then sat back happily in my seat while Pernfors consistently outplayed Becker on the long rallies and went on to win quite easily. Mark was very surprised and immediately curious, wanting to know how I had known what I did.

Not long after that encounter, the company that I was going to work for in London went bankrupt, leaving me stuck. I found some temporary work teaching tennis at a club where I bumped into Betsy [Nagelsen], Mark's wife, and mentioned what had happened when she asked why I was there. The next day she showed up at the club, and said that Mark wanted me to meet his two top guys. 'He thinks you'll be good at being a tennis agent as you seem to understand tennis,' she announced. If his senior colleagues had said no to me, I'm sure Mark wouldn't have bulldozed it through, although he did have a lot of influence. Either way, 30 years later I'm still working for IMG, so I guess he had a pretty good measure of whether or not I was suited to the job. Sometimes, trusting to instinct when it comes to recruitment can really work – for both parties.

Gavin Forbes

Look for the X factor

I was a law graduate fresh out of university in Belgium with big ambitions and an appetite for adventure. I knew that working as a lawyer in Belgium all my life would never be enough for me. I wanted something bigger and more international. I applied to be an intern in a London law firm although I hardly spoke a word of English. I was so keen to learn that I offered to help in any way I could, and if my performance wasn't good enough, I would even clean the windows or wash the floor. They agreed and then shortly afterwards, one of the partners came to me saying that their daughter was being unfairly treated by a Belgian bailiff. Could I help? I did, and he was very grateful. He asked what he could do to say thank you. I said: 'Just do me one thing. I have just filed some work for one of IMG's sports clients, and I am reading this book, *What They Don't Teach You at Harvard Business School*. Can you write me a note of recommendation?' I was fascinated by the company and wanted to be part of it.

The note was duly written and sent to IMG and shortly afterwards I received a phone call from Mark. He asked: 'Why should we hire you?' I said: 'I'll work for free; you pay me when I bring you some money.' That must have resonated with Mark, who was known to say to certain clients, 'pay me what you think I'm worth.' He saw a kindred spirit who was keen to get on, someone who was not only passionate, but who was prepared to go beyond expectation and move away from the norm. Now, when I interview people, I also ask: 'Why should I hire you? I need to understand what your X factor is. Not what is on your CV, what else is there?' It may not be in the management manual, but I believe it is an essential ingredient in building a corporate team that I will be able to trust and that will deliver.

Michel Masquelier

Hire in the expertise you need

In the modelling agencies in which I worked prior to IMG Models, the people running the company had an affiliation with the business. They wanted to be involved in all aspects of scouting and management, and pick up on the minutiae of my everyday work. At IMG Models it was completely different. Mark had realised early on that if you wanted to be global, you had to be involved in businesses that don't need a language to be understood. Very few things fit that bill – music, sports, and, he concluded, fashion. But apart from the fact that it could follow the same game plan, Mark had no idea about the business. The same could be said of my boss, Chuck Bennet, who took over the modelling division having been John McEnroe's manager. When Mark suggested to him that he should run IMG Models, Chuck pointed out that he didn't know a thing about it. 'Don't worry,' was the reply, 'you'll learn.' From a standing start, he picked up the business at lightning speed. As an agent he knew that he could hire models, but when it came to finding and developing models, Chuck knew he had no experience and made sure that he hired a core group of people who did. He could then layer his own sales and management expertise on top of his team's expertise in modelling to create a formidable division.

When I joined, I was given free rein to do what I wanted to do. No one has ever told me how to do my job, and that was part of the success. Within seven weeks of signing our first model at IMG in Paris, she was on the cover of Italian *Vogue*. That had never happened at IMG before. If you could bring money in and were performing, you were given a very long rope. It instilled huge confidence and belief and was the foundation on which IMG Models was built. There is no modelling agency that has been able to come close to our level of success. That came from the powerful combination of IMG's business savvy and trusting to industry expertise where it matters.

Jeni Rose

Keeping good staff

Mark did not give equity in the company, but he paid very well. A lot of very smart people stayed at IMG on that basis – it was great for your résumé and the pay was good. There was also a deferred compensation scheme – a bonus declared each year but payable over the following three years – that made it more difficult to leave.

But aside from monetary rewards, there were other factors at play. Mark was remarkable at holding onto people. He was excellent at working out what made people tick and what would excite them and make them loyal. That might be money, but it could also be global travel or winning industry awards. Anything that he could do that might help that person to keep score in their own personal way, he would.

Mark revelled in the continuity and extended tenure he created. It was obviously of value to the company to retain that experience and know-how, but he took great personal satisfaction in this too. When we had twice-yearly meetings of senior managers, the first informal item on the agenda was a roll call around the room of years spent at the company by each person.

Mark would positively glow as the numbers got higher each year. It wasn't a formal part of the meeting but Mark did nothing to stop it. He knew we would all talk about it afterwards. It would reinforce the message that we are all still here, having fun, and clearly this is the best place to be.

Alastair Johnston

Use your internal role models

In my third year at the helm of IMG Canada, we seemed to have hit a wall after two very strong years of growth. At a planning session for the upcoming year, Mark asked me why we weren't performing at the same level as Australia. In fact, he went further and said we were underperforming.

I suggested that perhaps I should travel to Australia and spend some time with the managing director, James Erskine. I could learn how he was enjoying this success and replicate it back in Canada. Mark loved the idea, but he thought it would make more sense for James to travel to North America, spend some time in New York and then a few days in Toronto with me and my team. He reasoned that James would have better input if he could observe first-hand what we were working on, how we were approaching the business and then offer real-time suggestions.

When James arrived he couldn't have been nicer, and I could see why he had been so successful. He exuded confidence in everything he did, from the way he commanded a room, to the way he dressed and spoke.

After two days of poring over pro-formas, reviewing upcoming projects and contrasting business development approaches, he declared, 'you need a Greg Norman', explaining that more than half of the revenue running through the Australian office was directly or indirectly tied to their representation of Greg's international rights.

Only in retrospect did I understand Mark's wisdom in

sending James to meet me in Canada (aside from the cost efficiencies, which Mark would never miss). As a trusted lieutenant, James would be able to report back to Mark on the performance of our office. But perhaps more importantly, he wanted me and everyone in the office to see how a successful international IMG managing director should look and act when outside his own environment. He knew the value of that first impression and the effect that his presence would have on me and on my young team. He surely knew that Greg Norman was the linchpin of the success in the Australian operation, but he needed me to hear that from someone who could deliver so many other unspoken messages.

Michael Wright

The value of a meritocracy

Under Mark, IMG operated as a meritocracy, with no salary structure or regimented job titles. Managers were told their budget for pay rises and it was left to their discretion as to how that was divided up. For the most part, job titles were not a big deal. I once had a new boss who was hired in from outside. He said that we must sort out titles and what broad pay range was appropriate for what title. It was a project we never finished as it was pushing custard uphill, and it didn't need to be done. There was no need to compare across divisions and try to force in a structure that didn't fit. In the middle of that project I attended a company meeting with a couple of outside speakers, including Eric Schmidt of Google. I remember him saying to the 200 or so of us present, 'I don't go in for titles in my company. I don't care if someone wants to put "rocket scientist" on their card. I just care about what they do.' It was a very pleasing moment.

The only titles that did create a bit of fuss were those that Mark handed out. In the early nineties, he started calling people vice president and senior vice president. Later on he added executive vice president. Those badges were highly prized. He did it to signal that some people were greater among equals and to repay loyalty. When I was a junior employee, working on company insurance, I received a company-wide memo from Mark announcing that three females had been made vice presidents. To see women recognised in that way was amazing. I remember feeling inspired and thinking I want to be one of them one day. It was the recognition that was important. People used to think it came with entitlement but actually it didn't, just some travel privileges. The most important thing was that it came from Mark and told everyone else that you were succeeding. And in a meritocracy, that recognition is hugely important.

Caroline Ward

SHORT SMART

If a member of staff has a list of items to discuss, deal with each point in isolation. There was no point telling Mark good news first so that you had equity before you moved on to the not so good things. There was no carried over equity. Everything was dealt with in isolation and totally on its merits. It took the emotion out of the discussion and made for a fair hearing – good for Mark, if less so for the bearer of news.

Ian Todd

Reacting to success and failure

Mark in many ways was a series of contradictions, but incredibly intelligent and forward-thinking contradictions. He was absolutely adamant about not wasting money on needless expense, and yet he would invest tens of millions of dollars in properties and projects with no immediate return if he believed he was building a valuable asset for the future.

It was not a good idea to let him catch you wasting money in any circumstance, as I once learned, but what I remember most was how he used what on the surface seemed like minor issues to teach bigger lessons.

Barry Frank, my boss at IMG at this time, and I had just returned from another one of his wildly successful Olympic negotiations where he managed to get NBC to sign a multimillion-dollar deal for the US television rights to the 1996 Summer Olympics in Atlanta. I remember sitting in Barry's office with anticipation, as we were told that Mark would be calling to congratulate us. Barry told me that he wanted me to pick up the extension because he wanted me to share in this moment of glory since this deal would pay millions of dollars in commissions to IMG. We were pretty full of ourselves at the time, full of self-congratulatory exuberance.

When the phone rang Barry kind of rubbed his hands together and said, 'This should be good.' He picked up the phone, and before Barry could even tell Mark that I was on the phone, Mark said, rather testily, 'Barry, do you know why Sean was staying in a suite at the Palace Hotel in Lausanne?' As I put the receiver down very gently, Barry said he would look into it. Needless to say we were pretty exasperated, but it was Mark's way of letting us know that, despite our huge success, he was also intent on making sure that we kept our perspective.

The point was that when you were a little too high on yourself, a little too taken with your recent big deal or believing your press clippings a little too much, that was precisely when you needed to be brought back down to earth. And no one did that better than Mark.

One of the reasons we accepted this kind of criticism was that he was fiercely loyal. We all saw Mark build up and support an executive who hadn't brought in a big deal for a while or someone who was down on his luck or discouraged. That was exactly the time when Mark was always there to build up your confidence, reminding us that we all go through rough patches and that he was 100 per cent behind you. Mark knew instinctively when you needed to be brought down a peg, but also when you needed a leg up. He was as good a friend and boss when you were down as when you were up.

And, later in my career, I would remind Mark, just for the record, that I was well aware of the corporate travel policy and that the upgrade to that suite was complimentary.

Sean McManus

A collaborative culture

If there was one thing that drove Mark to a complete fury it was a lack of communication between divisions to the detriment of the whole project. If he saw instances of un-joined up thinking, for example two people from licensing and sponsorship arriving for a meeting with one company at the same time, unbeknown to each other, there would be hell to pay.

It made everyone work much better together rather than competitively against each other. No business is without its ambitions, or people trying to unfairly claim credit to further their cause, but there was much less of that in IMG because people knew each other; and the culture, led from the top, was to collaborate.

People were colleagues, everyone from the highest to the lowest. It was important that everyone was made to feel that they were playing their part and that their part was important, whether they were the bookkeeper or the person putting up the signage. That culture was very important and it made people like and get on with each other and work as a team.

Job titles never meant anything particularly. The only time they were mentioned was when people working for me would say: 'I'm getting my business cards done, what shall I put on it? "Project manager"?' We used to think of things that would sound good, and that had a bit of clout to them. There was a hierarchy, but the significance of titles was to the outside world rather than your status internally.

Jeremy Palmer-Tomkinson

SHORT SMART

Be inclusive. I don't think I ever heard Mark once say 'I' rather than 'we'. He always made an inclusive presentation rather than 'I'm in charge and I have done that for you'. It is so important to make everyone in the team feel good and involved. I chair a charity committee, and I will go around the table during a meeting and ask the more silent members if they have anything they wish to add.

Buzz Hornett

Learn from the best

I am a reasonable tennis player and I would occasionally practise with Billie Jean King, who I represented. The thing that always struck me was how hard she worked after she had already won Wimbledon five times. I couldn't believe how she motivated herself to keep practising. I had been around sports all my life but not world champions. It changed my whole thinking about how hard you have to work and how much you have to prepare to be world class.

How often do you get to see that sort of thing in your twenties? If you are working for a company, you might work hard but you don't get to spend time with the real superstars in that industry. A 25-year-old at Microsoft does not get to hang out with Bill Gates that much. My exposure to Billie Jean made me realise that if I was going to be great at anything, I really had to go for it. It was a real eye-opener to me and inspirational. If you can learn from the best, it'll help you to understand what being the best really means.

Bob Kain

Pursue excellence

As president, I was responsible for William and Mary and I wanted to achieve the highest level of excellence, both for myself and for the college. To do that, you need exemplars and models. Mark [an alumnus] was an inspiration in that regard. He was always up to the mark and if something fell short he would want to know why and try to make it right.

Our women's tennis team is an example of that approach. Mark was responsible for the building of the McCormack-Nagelsen tennis facility, which is magnificent. Once it was completed he helped us to fill it with top tennis talent and become a national tennis power.

He helped us with equipment suppliers, recruiting people, hiring better coaches and finding others in the tennis community who could donate money to enhance the programme. He also helped us raise our profile. When we were trying to build the programme and get national visibility, we needed to schedule opponents. They were not always that interested in playing a team that didn't have a good record. But Mark would call the other athletic coaches and it would happen. We even took the team to Japan thanks to Mark's many tennis connections there.

We never won a national championship but came close on a number of occasions, and within four years we were playing at the very highest level, having come from nowhere. Without question that pursuit of excellence rubbed off on me. If you had a high-profile leadership job such as mine, and you spent a significant amount of time with someone like Mark, you always had the feeling that he was watching you, and you wanted to reach the same standards where only the best will do. Mark helped us prove we could play in the big leagues in fundraising, something that, if the money is used properly, is critical to excellence. It was Mark and his leadership that put us on that road, by setting his own standards and pursuit of excellence as the example.

Tim Sullivan

The value of being a good number two

It is important to know how to be a good number two and how to support the number one effectively. I think that Mark had this kind of relationship with Arnold Palmer and other clients, and was happy for them to take the limelight while he supported by keeping them centre stage.

I have spent a lot of time supporting other people, whether Paul Farmer at Partners in Health, J. W. Lee, the director general at the World Health Organization, or Michael Porter at Harvard Business School. Those years of being a dedicated number two have helped me in my role today. It was extremely helpful for me to be able to sit at the knee of great leaders and visionaries and fully dedicate myself to understanding and enabling their visions. Now that I'm in a top leadership role, I've done my best to turn that experience right around and ask myself every day: 'What can I do to help everyone around me be as productive as they can be? What can I do to remove obstacles to their success?' I tell my team that my job every day is to do the things that only I can do. If I do the things you can do, I am wasting my time and your time. As Garry Ridge, CEO of WD40 told me recently, as leaders, 'we're not here to grade their papers, we're here to help them get an A in the class.'

Jim Kim

Delegation breeds confidence

An important issue that Mark highlighted was the ability to delegate. As you become a leader of an organisation you have to be comfortable with delegating and with getting your satisfaction from watching others succeed. That can be a difficult transition for people to make. You can miss getting your hands dirty, and feeling that high when you complete a sales deal. The chances are that when you first take up a leadership role, you are much quicker at doing the job than the person you are leading. You have to resist the natural tendency to do it for them. It's an important lesson to have the confidence to be able to sit back and derive satisfaction from overseeing others.

It's something that I say to my colleagues who used to serve smaller clients but whose time is now taken up with serving larger clients. If a smaller client calls them about something, they know they could sort it really easily. But a better use of their time, and the company resources, is to have a junior colleague deal with whatever it is. I tell them that they should get used to saying the sentence, 'you don't want me for this, you want John in our company instead. He is really the expert, not me,' and to making the client feel good about the person you are putting forward.

Not only is it a better use of the senior colleague's time, it is important for the development of younger staff. You develop at a much slower pace and tend to relax as an employee if you think that someone else is going to come and sort something out. It's also demotivating to have a boss who keeps stepping back in. You have to make an employee feel comfortable about going out onto the thin part of the ice. They may get wet once or twice, but if that happens they should take comfort that they'll always get thrown a rope. Proper delegation breeds confidence at all levels of an organisation.

Peter McKelvey

How to delegate your most precious assets

As a company grows bigger, the founder will inevitably delegate more and more of the tasks that he used to undertake personally. Some will be more personal than others, and it is important to recognise that, and to ensure that the right information is passed on to guarantee a smooth transition.

As IMG grew, Mark knew that he would eventually need someone to assist with and ultimately assume the client relationship with Arnold Palmer. I knew what a fantastic opportunity this would be and how many doors it would open for my career, which proved to be the case. However, I was also aware of the importance of this particular client to Mark personally and to the company. The company had been founded on that original handshake with Arnold, and Mark was giving me, some immigrant kid from Scotland, the opportunity of a lifetime. It was quite daunting.

Mark was very generous with his help and gave guidance on what was important. Arnold needed to be able to find his own rationalisation as to why Mark was no longer dealing with him on a day-to-day basis. Mark pointed out that here was a more youthful, enthusiastic kid with fresh ideas who could also give more time to the relationship. It also meant that he and Arnold could become better friends again as there would be no awkward questions or asking him to do things he was reluctant to do. He told me to make sure that I also had the respect of Arnold's friends, as that would be important to Arnold who would have to explain to friends why Mark was not involved and I was.

Mark, of course, remained involved in major decisions. He simply explained that my job was to minimise the number of times Arnold would need to call him. He told me to just spend time with him in whatever way he wants. I was there to give him undivided attention, whether that was jogging together before breakfast, trips to the gym, or drinking beer at night. During those times, it was important to understand how to communicate and how not to communicate with Arnold. He warned me not to talk about golf. He might want to hear from someone about how good his golf had been at a particular tournament but it wasn't from me. If there was a button coming off one of his branded shirts and there was a way to fix it, that might be a conversation he would want to have, and that was how to get attention.

And that was how the relationship developed until, in the end, we continued to grow and expand our work for Arnold and his growing network of businesses while also growing IMG. We became great friends as well as business associates. But it was not a process that could have been rushed. All in all, the handover took five to six years. Succession planning in business relationships, as in organisational leadership, is too important to be left to chance, and often needs to take the time it needs to take.

Alastair Johnston

Trust in experience

Trust is the first thing you have to find between a customer and a supplier. It is harder when you first start out, but as you become more senior, there is no need to do business with people you don't like and don't trust. It was never an issue with Mark. He played an enormous role for The All England Lawn Tennis Club. We were all very naïve and no one had much experience, and we leaned on him. People felt we should manage IMG more than we did, but, like Mark, I'm a great believer in delegating and letting people who know what they are doing just get on with it, rather than looking over someone's shoulder all the time. Mark and IMG were at the forefront of the development of the business of sport. They had the knowledge and by trusting in them, we benefitted hugely.

There were also concerns that Mark might be promoting his own agenda. It didn't concern me. I think in life if you help someone, they will help you. I was confident that if Mark had ever got something out of Wimbledon, he would have squared that in his mind, and we would benefit at some point. And I would much rather people owe me than I owe them. Because the trust was there between us, we were happy to let the IMG team get on with the job.

John Curry

Managing egos

In a team environment, whether a sporting or a business context, there is no room for egos. With a few timely interventions, Mark was adept at keeping egos in check.

Accuracy in forecasting was one area in which he put this into practise. I was on the events management side of the business, where budgeting and forecasting were very important. Not surprisingly, there would be serious trouble for someone whose projection for an event was to make £1m and it had actually come in at a loss of £500k. However, Mark would be equally furious with anyone who said that they were going to make £100k and who actually made £500k. A big mallet would fall on their head within a nanosecond. The reaction would be: 'Don't come crowing to me about your great success. You should have said you were going to make this in all the forecasts.' The rebuke over lack of accuracy was enough to squash any inflated opinions of the success of the event.

Mark was also able to call on his 3 × 5 index cards in his pursuit of ego management. He would have a discussion with someone in which suggestions would be raised, questions asked and statements made. He would write it down as part of his record of the day. Six months later he would remember that conversation in all its detail. It meant that you would stick to the truth. It prevented people from boasting about what might happen, or saying that something had happened before it actually had. It meant that you cared, and you would try to stick to the detail. Following a conversation I once had with him, Mark went back to the US and said, 'I've heard from Jeremy that he did 25 events last year. That just doesn't sound right, will you check it out?' And some guy from the Cleveland office wrote to me asking exactly how many events I had run. So I wrote the list of events out and sent them back and heard nothing more. Mark clearly thought, 'Am I being spun a yarn?' and he made sure that he wasn't.

Jeremy Palmer-Tomkinson

See for yourself

At a small tennis club in Gastonia, NC, I met a young, tall-for-her-age, happy sixteen-year-old who hit bullets off both sides of the tennis court and spoke with a southern twang. It was Cory Ann Avants. I had read about Cory Ann in the local paper and made the trip to see her and meet her parents. She had guts and worked harder than any sixteen-year-old I had ever met. I was pretty excited when I went back and talked to the tennis division executives in Cleveland about her. Their suggestion was to get her down to the IMG Academy and have a hit with Nick Bollettieri. Then we would know what we had. After the session, Nick's evaluation was that Cory Ann had good foot movement, adequate speed, solid groundstrokes, a reasonable serve, and a big heart.

I never spoke with Mark about signing Cory Ann. The tennis division assigned Max Eisenbud, a young agent, to handle her work, the same agent that was attending tournaments with another IMG Academy talent, Maria Sharapova.

Shortly after she had been signed, Cory Ann was entered into the US Open tennis championships, and that was where I found Mark, hiding in plain sight. During the early rounds, Cory Ann was playing on Court number 14, a long way from Arthur Ashe Stadium Court. As she was getting prepared to serve I could make out Mark, sitting on his own across the court, scribbling notes on an index card.

It made an impression on me. Here was the most powerful man in tennis, sitting alone at a side court, watching a qualifying round. He wanted to see for himself if Cory Ann was the next Chris Evert – or just another talented kid.

Mark taught me street smarts that day. He trusted the tennis division to decide who to spend time checking out. He trusted Nick to evaluate the potential. He trusted Max to use exemptions into the main draw conscientiously. And he trusted me enough to manage the cost of spending time with an unknown by flying with her to New York to the US Open.

And then he showed up – hiding in plain sight – to see for himself. He would never circumvent agreed decision-making paths or try to undermine an executive. But he did want to stay involved. Mark keeping a low profile was a typical example of how to accomplish both objectives.

Michael Wright

3

People smarts in action

That is what street smarts really is – an applied people sense.

If *What They Don't Teach You …* taught us anything, it's that the **application** of street smartness is what matters in business. For MHM, this was about giving himself what he called a 'psychological edge' over others or to help him get the most out of others. Chapter 3 offers some concrete and practical examples of people smarts in action, featuring ideas and tools you can use to develop your own edge.

Much of MHM's philosophy around business life might be summarised in the three-tiered approach of what he called CADIF: *Commitment*; *Attention to detail*; and *Immediate follow-up*. A ruthless focus on effective and appropriate communication – both internal and external – was one of MHM's edge-builders, a straightforward and subliminal way of creating just the right impression. **Good communication is the life-blood of business**. It's essential to be professional in all your communications, from formal pitches or presentations to a routine internal email. This kind of detail really does make a difference.

MHM was just as ruthless about **the need to follow up and follow through**. Andy Pierce will never forget MHM's reaction to an occasion when he neglected to do so, learning the lesson that failing to get it right had the potential to reflect badly on the whole organisation's reputation for reliability: 'If you say it, you own it, and you have to follow through.' And as well as the importance of keeping your word, you'll also find many ideas for keeping in touch with the people you meet, from sending photographs of a time you spent together to the etiquette around entertaining.

Of course, this kind of attention to detail doesn't just happen; you need to have the tools in place to make it happen. Sarah Wooldridge, MHM's first London secretary and long-standing IMG staffer, gives us an insight into his 'organisation' system, based on those famous 3 × 5 cards, yellow legal pads and his 'Talk to' files – an early precursor of modern CRM systems. The message for all of us is simple: **to make the most of your people smarts, find and use the right CRM tools**. This will help you not just to find the right contacts, but also to make the most of them. Lisa Masteralexis' ability to rely on the alumni network at the University of Massachusetts is a great example of this.

'Don't be a time thief' is another MHM maxim that has resonated with his readers down the years. Again, it's all about the detail, and there is no doubt that efficiency impresses. **Keep to time, organise information so that's it's readily to hand, and learn how to master and give a clear brief**. Above all, don't waste people's time. Val Ackerman reflects on how disrespectful – as well as inefficient – it is to keep people waiting and also champions the skill of getting and keeping to the point: 'Setting time parameters is good business etiquette and can make dealings more efficient and productive for both parties.'

Respect is itself another people smart characteristic. **You have nothing to lose and everything to gain by treating people with respect**, especially those more junior than you. Bob Kain passes on a story from MHM himself about the ever-gracious Arnold Palmer tearing his young self off a strip for being unnecessarily heavy-handed with a locker room attendant. Former AELTC chairman John Curry also reminds us of the importance of respecting cultural differences, whether at home or abroad. Not everyone sees things from your own perspective; **respecting difference and the ability to walk in other people's shoes is another edge-builder**.

People smarts can also be applied to techniques for looking after yourself, for making sure that you keep yourself fighting fit and game-ready. Tennis legend Billie Jean King shows us how the routines and rituals employed by top sports stars have a place in all our lives, while MHM's daughter, Leslie McCormack Gathy, suggests that her father was practising mindfulness long before it became popular. **Find your own strategies for coping with the pressures of business life and keep an eye on well-being and work-life balance**. You'll need all the smarts you can muster to be on top of your game when the chips are down.

Are you ready to apply those people smarts? Here we go.

Communicate, communicate, communicate

Within every company there is untapped potential that is lost unless people communicate with each other. With effective communication, dots can be connected, and solutions appear out of nowhere.

Mark had very little tolerance for lack of communication. The message was reinforced on an almost daily basis to communicate in any way possible – by fax, by phone, by letter – with all divisions within the company. We even had a meeting of senior people once or twice a year to which the perceived leaders from the next generation were invited in order that they too could start joining in the conversations.

Because of this focus, people did communicate, and would connect the dots. The opprobrium for not sharing information was so institutionalised by Mark that it happened naturally.

As a CEO, I now see the effort required to get people to communicate and the inertia that I need to overcome, and it drives me crazy. Every day that goes by I have more respect for what Mark accomplished.

I talk about connecting the dots at every meeting. In this age, when people are inundated with messages, we are conditioned to under-communicate. But things that you might not think are relevant may well be relevant to someone else, so the default position should be over-communication. We don't give each other enough credit for being able to weed out the irrelevant. The person who receives the information is far better equipped to work out its relevance than you. How could you know? Communicating thoroughly and effectively is crucial and something I think about all the time.

Andy Pierce

The art of email

Mark did not have to grapple with the blessing and the curse that email represents, but his views on the importance of professionalism in any communication still apply, regardless of the medium. Mark talked about the precision with which he edited letters, and the same is true of email. Each email is a reflection of your intelligence and thoroughness and a chance to clarify and advance your business position. Sending unchecked, sloppily written, grammatically incorrect email can be harmful to your image and can alter your effectiveness in the business world.

Email etiquette matters. People expect a rapid response and if you're sure about your position, it's best to give as prompt a reply as possible. That said, people send emails at all hours of the day and night, which can create unnecessary work and anxiety for the recipient. Generally, a work email is best sent during a workday unless urgent. I won't send a business email over the weekend unless it is time-sensitive and absolutely necessary. People – both the sender and the recipient – need to take time off and to recharge, and time away from the inbox is one way to help.

Care needs to be taken as to the content of emails. Email is toneless so there is a premium on communicating in a clear way and eliminating the nuance that can lead to confusion or hard feelings. I am not a fan of exclamation marks. Emails may not stay private, so restraint is best. If your note says something you wouldn't want to see on the front page of the newspaper, you should probably not write it. Escalation of emotion by email is also inadvisable. If you receive an email written in anger, responding with anger can only make matters worse. There is a moment, very early on, when ranting needs to stop and a call or meeting becomes the best (and only) way to work out the issue.

Emails make business dealings more efficient and allow business professionals to get more work done. However, electronic communication should never be a complete substitute for verbal conversations or personal interactions. Emails are vital, but only as part of a wider business communication mix: never forget the power and importance of handwritten notes, phone calls and face-to-face meetings.

Val Ackerman

SHORT SMART

My dad was a stickler for getting people's names spelled properly. He would always make sure that this was checked and double-checked. If he made a mistake, he was quick to apologise for the mistake the next time he wrote to the person. From one who regularly gets her name spelled wrong, especially in the UK, I know first-hand how jarring it can be to have your name written incorrectly. Getting it right can make all the difference in how a correspondence is received.

Leslie McCormack Gathy

The power of a personal follow-up

To this day, I try my best to embrace lessons I learned from Mark, including his policy of personal follow-up after meetings and calls of any kind. With hindsight – usually the clearest view of all – I can see that he used those devices to help in negotiations, but never to the detriment or humiliation of others.

One example involves an immensely talented professional woman golfer who had faced struggles in her personal life but who Mark never abandoned or declared 'too much trouble'. After a meeting to discuss a particular deal, he asked me to stay and talk, and then proceeded to share her story with me.

It was important to Mark that I understand both her talent and her tribulations. He asked me to consider her for an on-air role at the Women's British Open. The next morning a concierge knocked on my hotel-room door and presented me with a copy of her autobiography, sent over by Mark. It was his way of making sure that I knew the whole story. I read the book, learned a great deal, and it became an important component in making a deal for her. Mark's attention to people, relationships and detail often proved to be uncanny.

Another time, Mark had invited me to lunch at Wimbledon, but I had no idea who the other guests would be. When I arrived I joined a table with several guests – including a man named Nando Parrado.

Nando fascinated me. He was the Uruguayan rugby player portrayed by Ethan Hawke in the movie *Alive*, based on the book about a rugby team stranded by a plane crash in the Andes. I had seen the movie and was awed by the team's incredible struggle to survive, their raw and stubborn will to live. Nando was, and is, an accomplished motivational speaker whom IMG represented. The lunch discussion was wide-ranging and fascinating, and my head was spinning when I arrived back in my hotel room afterwards. Once again Mark had shared not just 'contacts' but relationships. And of course when I got back to my hotel, waiting there, courtesy of Mark, was a copy of the book version of *Alive*.

It seems incredible to me now that I only knew Mark for a few years, because he had such an impact on me and on my relationships with others. His personal touch, and the intuitive way he dealt with people are invaluable commodities that I will always admire and cherish – and, I hope, continue to put to good use.

Mark Lazarus

Keep your word

If you say it, you own it, and you have to follow through.

I had been at IMG for twenty years when I had a call from Mark, who thundered down the line, 'I am as disappointed in you right now as I have ever been.' I almost fell out of my chair. What could I have done?

It turned out that two weeks before, I had had lunch with Mark and the CEO of Hertz in Mark's favourite restaurant in New York. Our guest had commented on how much he liked both the restaurant and the table that we were sitting at, and said that he thought it would be ideal for his board meeting in a couple of weeks' time. I had said, 'leave it with me, I'll make sure you get it,' and then I had completely forgotten to do anything about it.

If something had gone wrong on a contract or we had lost a client, either of which would, in a material sense, have had a more significant impact on the company, Mark would in all probability have said never mind, don't worry. But saying something and not following up was unforgiveable. When people said or represented something, it became a representation of all of IMG and if it then wasn't kept, it became a negative reflection on the whole company. There were a lot of people at IMG, and our reputation was dependent on each of us keeping our word in every situation. The importance of following up on representations made – no matter how small – was a very valuable lesson that I continue to pass on.

Andy Pierce

SHORT SMART

Mark always kept to the right time. If he said he'd call at 3 p.m., he did. Being able to rely on that showed that he valued us as a client. If he hadn't called when he said he would we might have thought he had other things on his mind and we had slipped down the pecking order in terms of his priorities.

Chris Gorringe

Efficiency impresses

I once mentioned in conversation with Mark that when I was a boy golfer there had been a UK player called Peter Townsend who was the best player around at that time. Mark took note of what I said, even though it was not a business conversation. Within half a day, he had found a letter that he had written to the US Tour 40 years before saying what a good player Townsend was and that he should be playing on their tour. The point itself was trivial but it served several purposes. Firstly, it showed that Mark had been paying attention to everything that I said. It also showed his deep understanding and insight into the game that Townsend had been on his radar so long ago. Finally, the fact that his organisational skills were such that he could lay his hands on a letter written 40 years ago so quickly was staggering. It was impressive.

Peter Dawson

The importance of a clear brief

At one stage Mark was leading negotiations for the European broadcast rights for Wimbledon and I was brought in as a junior lawyer to help. It was about 5 p.m. Friday and I was wrapping up for the weekend. Just as I was about to go, the phone rang. It was my boss saying, 'Timo, we have a problem. McCormack is flying in at 7 a.m. Monday morning and he wants contracts for the ancillary rights. You must have them ready for 9 a.m. Monday.' And that was it. He went off for the weekend as I sat there wondering what on earth I should do. I got in touch with another colleague who very kindly came in on Saturday morning and gave me a 40-minute briefing, as I had no idea what was required. My boss had just passed Mark's message onto me without giving me any context. I worked through Saturday and Saturday night without sleeping and then Sunday. It took me the best part of 40 hours, but in the end I was quite pleased with what I had achieved as I handed them over.

Later that morning I was summoned to a meeting and was expecting a pat on the back for the hard work I had put in. But instead, Mark was not best pleased and let it be known. Why, he wanted to know, had we written incredibly long contracts when all he wanted was three short side letters? Utterly deflated, I walked out with my tail between my legs, but having learned two important lessons. The first was the importance of keeping things short and precise, but also that I should have nailed my boss on exactly what Mark wanted. If I had had the right briefing, the task probably would have taken around four hours not 40, and I might even have got that pat on the back. The importance of giving – and receiving – a clear brief was a valuable lesson to learn.

Timo Lumme

Breaking bad habits

Bad habits can be hard to break if they are ingrained. One way around the problem is to put up additional barriers that make people stop and think.

My father would frequently scrutinise company expenditure. After one such inspection, he sent a memo addressed to worldwide employees, which simply said: 'From this point forward the company will no longer pay for overnight shipping of letters and packages. Of course, if there is a very unusual circumstance where overnight delivery is essential please write to my assistant and she will approve each request on a case by case basis.'

This two-sentence memo saved IMG over $250,000, an almost 80 per cent reduction in overnight shipping from the year before the memo was sent. He, of course, told his assistant to approve any request that came her way. However, the mere fact that someone had to call her first meant that the executive team quickly corrected their bad habits and only sent things overnight that were critical to business. The simple act of adding that additional step put a stop to unthinking actions that had become habits and made an immediate difference.

Todd McCormack

Don't underestimate the power of the diary-keeper

When you need to see a senior executive urgently, often the only people who can make that happen are their PAs.

When Sky merged with BSB to form BSkyB, the new company was led by Sam Chisholm, a man legendary for his abrasive manner, and no fan of ours. However, he was going to be an important contact for us, so I followed Mark's example of making sure that I had a friendly relationship with his PA. Quite a bit later it was time to renegotiate the European Tour's TV contract with Sky. It was an important contract, worth a lot of money, and it needed to be finalised as a matter of urgency. However, Sam was in the US for two weeks on a roadshow. I spoke to his PA and explained that I really needed to see him. She said that his diary was absolutely blocked, and that would have been that for most people. However, I persisted, and because of the relationship we had developed over time, I managed to squeeze myself into a breakfast meeting at 6.30 a.m. one morning. We met at a hotel and got the deal done. That would never have happened had his PA not been willing to help me. Always be nice to the people around the person you are trying to get to. Not only is it common courtesy, but they often control more than you think they do.

Ian Todd

Have the right CRM systems in place

Customer Relationship Management (CRM) is an established business concept these days, but without the right systems to back it up it remains just a concept. In the days before computers, Mark devised his own.

I was Mark's first London secretary, working at IMG since the mid-1960s and so was closely involved with his system of capturing personal information via the 3 × 5 index cards he always carried in his pocket and his legal yellow pad pages on which he recorded his diary, written in pencil.

He had two other secretaries based in Cleveland, Ohio and New York and, without the internet or mobile phones, we would hold secretarial summits once or twice a year so that we could work through pages and pages of his global contacts to share information and update our records. This must have been one of the very first CRM systems, as we added personal notes to each contact about whether they received his Golf Annual, Christmas cards and presents, their birthdays etc.

When Mark telephoned me from wherever he was in the world, his 3 × 5 cards meant that he would never forget anything, so I had no way of missing anything – or was in trouble if I had. And when he arrived in London for his regular visits, he would have a huge pile of UK paperwork to go through with me; he just loved handing it all over for immediate action and for his 'Talk to' files, so called because they included all the relevant documents for the next conversation.

His systems were so bulletproof that most of his executives and staff copied them, to the extent that this early version of a CRM system, led by Mark and operated by his colleagues, became a crucial part of IMG's success. His vision of a joined-up, global system for having the right information in place at the right time was the key to doing business, and remains so for any client-facing business today.

Sarah Wooldridge

Don't waste people's time

Mark was a big believer in not being a time thief, and it is a sentiment that resonates strongly with me. Being on time is critical in the business world. It is a sign of respect to not keep people waiting. It is imperative to let the other person know if you are running late for a meeting, and inexcusable not to, given how easy it is to send a text or email with a heads-up and an apology.

I was once due to meet a colleague for lunch, and arrived at the restaurant at 12.30 p.m., the time we had arranged. When she hadn't arrived by 12.45 p.m., I texted her and discovered that she was still very far away. When she didn't show up by 1 p.m., I texted her to say that I could no longer wait and we would have to reschedule. It took her a year to work up the courage to call me to rearrange. I agreed to it but insisted that the meeting be at my office. That way if she was running late again, I could at least get other work done while I was waiting. There were certain topics I wanted to discuss with her, so a meeting was still of interest to me. But, given the history, it needed to be on my terms.

Not wasting people's time by getting to the point is also important. If I am scheduling a phone call, I generally allow 30 minutes. If the person on the other end is rambling on for twenty minutes and we still haven't got to the point of the call, I will say that I've got another call or meeting in ten minutes, so what can I help you with in these last ten minutes? It is not only efficient but good manners to reconfirm at the beginning of the call how much time both parties have set aside. The same applies with a business meeting. I will usually say at the beginning, 'I hope my assistant told you that unfortunately I only have half an hour,' in order to establish the ground rules up front. It is not rude to be direct. Rather, if done courteously and politely, setting time parameters is good business etiquette and can make dealings more efficient and productive for both parties.

Val Ackerman

Stronger together

When *What They Don't Teach You at Harvard Business School* hit the market, the Sport Management Department at the University of Massachusetts, Amherst, adopted the book as required reading for students, me included. It became my business bible. The concepts that stuck with me were the value of having a law degree within the business world, that learning by doing was a more effective way to enhance classroom learning, and that business success in large part came down to common sense and a willingness to work hard. But what most resonated was the concept of having good people sense. Now, as an associate professor of sport management and an associate dean within the Isenberg School of Management, I see the same lessons being taught to today's students.

Building a strong and authentic network takes work. It involves getting to know people. It means taking a genuine interest by asking questions and actively listening to responses, following up, sharing, and being a giver rather than a taker. If one gives unconditionally, in time a virtuous circle of giving will be created, and we all benefit. Our 7,000-strong McCormack Department of Sport Management alumni network has been cultivated for close to 50 years, starting with Tom Peters, the first alumnus in 1972. Alumni give back by mentoring students, visiting our classrooms to share insights, and providing internship and job opportunities. Our students are told about the power of our network, but seeing it in action is what sticks with them.

Its power was demonstrated when, in 2012, one of our students wanted to bring a baseball general manager in as a guest speaker. I said, why just one, we have three alumni who are GMs, an honour and a distinction for our programme given that a GM is one of the most prestigious and sought-after positions in the US sports industry. With one call from us, Chris Antonetti of the Cleveland Indians, Ben Cherington of the Boston Red Sox, and Neal Huntington of the Pittsburgh Pirates took time from their busy schedules to return to campus and share their experiences. They enthusiastically gave their time because someone had done so for them. They were paying it forward and I believe, in time, the students in that packed auditorium that night will do the same when they receive a similar call for assistance and insight.

I firmly believe that our collective success is driven by helping each other become successful. We can bask in one another's glory, not just our own. We are stronger together than apart.

Lisa Masteralexis

Lessons from the locker room

Fairly early on in their relationship, Arnold Palmer and Mark were out playing golf. After they had finished, they went back to the changing rooms for a shower. Once they had spotted that there were no towels, Mark started shouting for the locker room attendant. When he failed to materialise, Mark got more and more angry, so that by the time he finally did arrive with the towels, Mark really let go, shouting at him for having been so slow. The attendant shrank away into the background. Mark and Arnold carried on getting dressed and Arnold, as they were leaving the locker room and walking out, said to Mark: 'I don't treat people that way. If you are going to represent me and manage me in my career, you can't treat people that way either.'

Years later, Mark would happily tell that story. He used to say it was a great lesson in the way you treat people, and one that he wanted to pass on to others. Arnold was the 'king', but he treated everyone the same, always with respect and never by talking down to them. To Mark, who was a cocky young agent at the time, it was an early lesson, and one that left a huge impression.

Bob Kain

Defend the little guy at meetings

There was a former tennis player who went on to hold a position with Tennis Australia, who was particularly difficult to work with. We had dealings with Tennis Australia through our representation of the Australian Open, and used to meet as a group probably three times a year.

At one of these meetings I had to give a presentation about a new television rights agreement. Except for not getting customers to pay for their commentary positions, it covered everything that Tennis Australia wanted, and so there should have been a lot of contented faces. This representative, however, did not see it that way, and when I mentioned the commentary positions, started screeching at me in a very aggressive manner. The language was harsh and the attack was personal. I was shocked, but before I could figure out how best to respond, Mark stopped him in his tracks, asking: 'Have you ever served a double fault and then gone on to win the match? I think Buzz has just done that.'

It was astonishing. He went very quiet after that. I will always remember that moment and when I am in meetings, I will defend the person who may not be the most important in the room from attacks from those more senior.

Buzz Hornett

SHORT SMART

My grandfather learned much about dealing with people by watching Arnold Palmer. I have been equally fortunate to work with and learn from Roger Federer. One lesson took place at the US Open. After playing a late-night match and a further hour of press interviews, Roger finally left the stadium at 1.30 a.m. Outside, there were a number of fans who had waited for him. Since he had another match the next day, I was sure he'd head straight for his car, but instead he patiently signed every autograph, posed for selfies and chatted amicably. It wasn't an act. He knew that his fans were a large part of his success and he was grateful to them. One of Roger's favourite quotes is: 'It is nice to be important, but it's more important to be nice.'

Chris McCormack

The tactical coincidence

When I was president of ABC Sports, Mark invited me over to be his guest at Wimbledon. I knew Mark well from having started my career at IMG, and I had just re-engaged with him through the negotiations for ABC's coverage of the British Open. I remember that at the time the US rights to Wimbledon, held by NBC, were about to expire.

I was thrilled to be going to Wimbledon, and was very much looking forward to the day, particularly watching the tennis from the Royal Box. Mark arranged for a car to pick me up from my hotel and take me straight to his marquee for lunch. It was a very pleasant meal with good company, but after a while I kept looking at my watch because I wanted to be in the box in time to watch the matches and didn't want to be late. Quite bizarrely, Mark didn't seem bothered or anxious at all and things were moving along at a very casual, leisurely pace. Just as I was trying to fathom out what on earth was going on, one of Mark's employees came up and whispered something in his ear. Just like that, lunch ended and Mark swept me out of the marquee.

As we emerged, who should walk out of the NBC marquee directly opposite but Dick Ebersol, chairman, and Ken Schanzer, president of NBC Sports. Mark put on an Oscar-winning performance of feigning surprise, and did the introductions all round. He even had someone take a picture of us in front of the NBC marquee. And it was then that I knew that Mark had brought me to Wimbledon for precisely that moment. He just wanted NBC to know that ABC was interested in acquiring the Wimbledon rights. It was a subtle message he was able to deliver by controlling everything that he controlled and in masterminding a very useful – if tactical – coincidence.

Howard Katz

How to entertain

Mark used to come to South Africa every year before going out to the Australian Open. I had a place in Cape Town and I invited him to stay there each year on his way to Australia. One year we were at Wimbledon together and he mentioned that, sadly, he was not going to be able to go to my estate any more as they had moved the date of the Australian Open. Now that it was in January, he wouldn't be able to come to the house beforehand, as I would be there, spending Christmas and New Year with my family. I said that if he did come out, I could always build a guest house. We carried on chatting and I forgot about the conversation. I next saw him at the US Open at the end of August. I asked him again if he was coming to Cape Town or not, because it was getting close to Christmas. He said, 'I tell you this, Sol. If you can build a guest house between now and Christmas, I'll definitely come out.' I said that's fine, and we built the cottage in three months. Sure enough, Mark would stay there every year, and wherever else I saw him, he would ask, 'how's my house in Cape Town?!'

He had no problem in repaying that hospitality. I would be with him for the last four days of Wimbledon, and always the finals of the French Open at Roland Garros. Mark's 'marquee' at Roland Garros was in the gardens opposite the venue. In fact it wasn't a marquee at all. Mark explained that in the heat of a disagreement with the French Tennis Federation (FFT), the FFT ejected IMG from their Corporate Hospitality Village. Undeterred, and through a contact with the then Mayor of Paris, Jacques Chirac, IMG hired the two massive nineteenth-century glasshouses inside the city's botanical garden right across the street from Roland Garros. One was used as a relaxed space for IMG's tennis clients and their families. The larger greenhouse was transformed into an elegant, spacious corporate hospitality area that became the envy of any visitor to the French Open. You can imagine Mark's glee when several years later the FFT tried, unsuccessfully, to hire the botanical garden space out from under IMG's nose. Now that's when you know you're entertaining well.

Sol Kerzner

SHORT SMART

Creating the right atmosphere for a business lunch is very important. Mark insisted on checking a restaurant before booking a table and finding a quiet area with no music where it would be easier to hear the conversation. Other tips were to make the booking for three people even if there will only be two of you – you will be given a larger table with greater space between you and other restaurant diners. Sit facing the room in order that your guests are not distracted by events elsewhere in the restaurant. If the meal is a success, take note of the table number for future reference.

Sarah Wooldridge

Stay culturally attuned

The ability to operate in different cultural settings is a skill that not everyone has, and picking the right people to represent you abroad is very hard. Recruiting people who are good but will also fit into your organisation is hard enough; recruiting for abroad adds another layer of complexity. I have built international businesses and I have put good people in foreign countries and they have not done well. It is amazing how fast Mark built IMG around the world. He was exceptionally good at picking good people, and if he had to make changes, he would do so quickly. That differentiates good people. We all make the same number of mistakes – the trick lies in acknowledging them and making changes quickly.

To be successful abroad, you need to be able to read and respond to the cultural differences. Mark travelled well. I saw him in many different environments and he was able to get on with French people, Germans, Japanese, whoever. The differences can be complex. In Japan, for example, Mark was a lot less forward than he was in his office in Cleveland. He would be more deferential while being encouraging, but he was also the showman in terms of making clear decisions. Customers wanted to see clarity in decision making and to see that they were dealing with the top person, but they also did not want the feeling that they were being told what to do. Back at home, Mark would not be deferential but was always happy to delegate and for others to be seen to be making the decisions. Both as an owner and a manager, it is important to be able to respond to what is required in different situations. Always stay attuned to the importance of culture – both at home and abroad.

John Curry

Dealing with pressure

People who are at the top of what they do, you see their brain ticking over all the time. Mark was always conceptualising, thinking how can we get that situation, that comment, whatever, to work to our advantage. His brain never stopped. I have a saying about bringing all of yourself all of the time. You have to bust your chops every day, all of the time. You can't just do it once a week and then switch off, especially if you own a company or are in a senior position. That responsibility never leaves your brain and stays with you every night before going to sleep. To cope with that pressure, you first of all have to enjoy it. You have to be able to think, 'This is good, and whatever I experience today I will learn from it and it will make me better.' Secondly, you have to have a routine. If you watch any top athlete in whatever sport, you will spot that they have their rituals and routines that, if not followed, will upset their rhythm and affect performance.

You see it in the way that tennis players go through the same rituals on the tennis court. Coaches teach us to do that. It instils inner rhythm, calm and peace. It is the sameness that allows you to be calmer. You are always adapting to what is going on externally, all around you. If you can get yourself organised internally and find that calm, it gives you the greatest chance to do your best. You see it in the way players bounce the ball the same number of times before a serve. Or the way that they leave a towel in the same place at each change of ends. You only have a few seconds when you're changing ends, so you had better have everything where you need it and not have any reason to panic. As with a player, so with executives facing stress and pressure in their daily work lives. Mark knew that having his routines worked for him. That was why he had his 3×5 cards in his top pocket, every hour of every day, ready to take notes on anything of interest. It was why he set such store by his yellow legal pads on which he had recorded his daily 'to do' lists. And it was why he scheduled in his power naps during the day. They were all part of the coping mechanisms, the rituals and routines that helped him cope with pressure, and gave him the inner calm required to face each day's challenges.

Billie Jean King

Practise mindfulness and well-being

There are countless examples of the strict principles my dad applied to his business life. What truly astounds me is how ruthless he also was in managing the schedule for his personal life, health and well-being. I am convinced his business success is integrally linked to the constant care and attention he paid to this area.

My dad applied the art of mindfulness and well-being 50 years before it was fashionable to do so. He tracked the number of hours he slept, his weight and the amount of exercise he took each day and analysed his year-on-year results. Daily slots for naps and exercise and longer, restorative health breaks were scheduled just like any business meeting. He could compartmentalise with great skill. I don't believe he ever fell victim to endless hand-wringing over a difficult problem. Rather, he would estimate how long it might need to resolve and schedule a window of time during which he would worry about it. Likewise, he loved to schedule 'creative thinking' sessions and kept a list of projects and ideas to ponder when he had time to think and reflect.

The ability to focus on one thing at a time and then close the box and move on is a great skill. It allows you to maximise both productivity and relaxation. The flip side of scheduling to this degree is that you lose spontaneity. My dad's diary was a well-oiled machine and God help those who interfered with it. He was blessed with excellent support staff who helped him adhere to his strict schedule. Not many of us have such luck and, as we all know, sometimes life intervenes.

Before my wedding, the father of the bride requested I write him a memo outlining what he needed to do over the course of the wedding celebrations. I wrote up three pages explaining what pre-wedding events were planned, their timings and the cast of characters who would be at each. I neglected, however, to write about one important detail that I thought was self-evident. Standing at the door of the church watching the bridesmaids disappear down the aisle, my dad pulled out his memo looking for confirmation of what he was to do next. Not entirely surprised, I slipped my arm through his and guided him into the church.

I certainly learned from my father the benefits of planning a schedule. However, from my mother, Nancy, who is not always the best timekeeper and who relishes a bit of spur-of-the-moment activity, I was also taught that spontaneity can reap enormous benefits. As I go about my life, I try to strike the right balance.

Leslie McCormack Gathy

> **SHORT SMART**
>
> When you are served a meal on a plane, the temptation is to keep on picking away at it long after you are full, until the tray is removed. Mark said to me, put your napkin over the tray, tuck it in, and then you won't pick anymore. I do it all the time on long flights.
>
> *Neil Hobday*

Go that extra mile

Praising people for doing a good job is appropriate in some circumstances (or with certain types of people) but in other cases it can lead to complacency. This was certainly Mark's view, whose pats on the back and praise were extremely hard to come by.

I was working in the IMG Cleveland office one day when Mark strode in without warning. He said: 'Dick, you have to do something very important for me. Arnold [Palmer] is mad at me, and I want to be able to give him a cheque for $100k. I'm seeing him in three days, so you need to have it by then.' With that, he closed the door and left me to it. I had no idea how I was going to get $100k in three days. I started fishing around blindly hoping something would catch and ended up talking to someone who found athletes to do promotions on a one-off basis. He had a client that made photocopiers, who was happy to pay for a picture of Arnold copying a book about golf. I explained that it had to be done as soon as possible and that I would need the cheque within three days.

The shoot was done and the cheque arrived two days later – for $85k, as the agent had taken 15 per cent commission. I still thought it was pretty impressive given the time constraints I had, and went in and proudly presented it to Mark. Instead of sharing my delight that I had managed to turn something around so quickly, he came back and said 'Dick, you couldn't even ask for the other 15k?'

I might have been frustrated at the time that my efforts had gone unrewarded but it reinforced the point that, given Mark's exacting standards, nothing less than my best would be good enough. I learned that going that extra mile, even under pressure, is the key to business excellence and success.

Dick Alford

Work-life balance in a 24/7 world

Mark always advocated taking an interest in people's families. He himself skilfully blended business and family. Once when I was a guest at his house on Maui when his entire family was there, I wandered in from the beach and he was meeting in the family living room with two leading figures in surfing and assessing whether there was a role for IMG to take in that sport – this in full view and earshot of his family. The surfing guys were gracious to the family, and to me. No one viewed it as an intrusion of Mark's business life into his personal life, or vice versa. Those lives were integrated. There is so much talk today about work-life balance, but the notion of compartmentalising your work life and your personal life in order to achieve that balance becomes ever more outdated, now that so many professions demand 24/7 attention.

In this regard, Mark was ahead of his time. He not only integrated his professional life and his family life, but he saw the value in doing so. People get to know you better if they see you with your family. It can be a real ice-breaker. They realise that the person with whom they are dealing is not duplicitous – is not putting on an act just for business purposes – and so there is a greater level of trust. Conversely, Mark's then adolescent children saw him in action and were able to appreciate that he was the same guy on the job as he was at home. I have seen this dynamic in the arc my own life has taken. I attend a number of legal conferences each year, but the one I make sure never to miss is a media law conference held annually, usually in Florida. There is a tradition of taking families along. There are people in the media world who I came to know – or know better – through their families. And they came to know me better in the same way. It really enhances relationships. And business is founded on relationships and trust.

Bob Latham

Good advice never gets old

I was drawn to the University of Massachusetts partly because the sports management programme was based in the business school and partly because of their focus on real world experiences, interpersonal relationships, and entrepreneurialism. I was a student during the time that the department became the Mark H. McCormack Department of Sport Management. We learned a lot about him and his principles and his focus on people, and were inspired to follow in that same spirit of entrepreneurship and growth.

I joined the Association of Diversity in Sport, and in my second year we built a career fair on campus. We thought that getting in front of companies and being able to create a first impression rather than just sending a résumé was even more relevant in our people-centric industry than for accounting and finance types. We recruited twenty organisations in our first year, which extended to 40 organisations, keynotes and panel series discussions by the second year. We sold what we had – our students – pointing to the value of securing talent for internships or entry-level positions. Now I have my dream entry-level job working in the basketball industry. I am part of a group with a clear global and entrepreneurial outlook. I have travelled around the world and in many ways my role feels like being part of a start-up within a much larger conglomerate.

It's funny that *What They Don't Teach You at Harvard Business School* is more than 30 years old. From my experience, there's not a single piece of it that doesn't apply, particularly in terms of building genuine friendships and relationships. I have co-founded a networking group for the sports industry, with the aim of connecting and reconnecting with people in New York. I was approached by one of my mentors with the idea as we were struggling to keep in touch. The goal was for us to get together and catch up, and bring a few others along. It has grown organically and we now have 400 people on our database after just one year. The philosophies around relationships that I learned while studying and that were espoused over 30 years ago are still just as valid, both for me and for those around me, in our working lives.

Melcolm Ruffin

PART 2

Negotiation

4

Preparing to negotiate

*I often see negotiation as the last step in an ongoing
sales effort, the culmination of a process that
may have lasted several months or more.*

For MHM, one of the biggest gaps in a Harvard Business School
education was a lack of focus on selling. The sales and negotiating tips at the core of *What They Don't Teach You ...* aimed
to rectify this by sharing what he considered to be the essence
of effective selling: timing, patience and persistence coupled
with a sensitivity to the situation and the person you're dealing
with. He also believed that a good healthy dose of common sense
could make all the difference. So there is hope for even those of
us with a limited grasp of how to negotiate and sell, and who feel
the fear of putting ourselves out there. Part 2 offers a masterclass
on negotiation from the people who learned from the master
himself.

This first chapter focuses on approaches to, and preparation for, negotiation. President of ESPN, John Skipper, identifies
the IMG way of negotiating as a 'common-sense, philosophical
method of getting results for your company and your clients', a
philosophy he himself is happy to espouse. Adopting **a problem-
solving, consultative approach to negotiation and selling is
much more likely to give you the results you want** – and open
the possibility of more lasting business relationships. Former
Playboy chairman and CEO, Christie Hefner, characterises the

art of negotiation as 'the ability to understand the other sides' needs, wants, worries and desires in order to come together around a vision and structure that is a win-win.'

Negotiating partners can be 'read' just like individuals. You need to get to know the organisations you want to deal with and the people who are their representatives. **Work backwards from the challenges your negotiating partner is facing and look to present them with opportunities or solutions that will work for them.** Understand where the real strength lies in any negotiation, as Ian Todd shows us with his account of the America's Cup negotiations. Take the time to find the right gatekeeper or advocate who will help you learn what you need to know to help your cause. And, crucially, be aware of who does the buying and what the buying process will be.

As Stacey Allaster of the Women's Tennis Association (WTA) so eloquently advocates, the most effective negotiators and sellers know, and have passion for, the product or service they're offering. You also need to anticipate objections or barriers. **Tone and context matter too.** Set the scene positively from the outset, assuming that the deal will be done. Be candid and conciliatory to keep things moving. Keep an eye on the practicalities: follow up in writing once a deal is done or to clarify mid-negotiation and tie everything up as soon as possible once you've agreed.

Values and ethos also have an important role to play. Bring your own to the table, and understand and respect the values that are important to the other side. Michael Wright shows how honesty can, as in so many other contexts, be the best policy in a negotiation. John Curry is clear that MHM's respect for Wimbledon's heritage and tradition, which led it 'to behave in a way that embodied [its] values', was essential to IMG doing business with and for them. Neil Hobday and Guy Kinnings are both insightful about the need to balance the commercialisation of sport with respect for its own special spirit.

Even with the best preparation and the right insights, there are, of course, times where sheer persistence will be the only way to break through. Jeremy Palmer-Tomkinson gives us an object lesson in not taking no for an answer. MHM and IMG's pursuit of the UK's Royal Horticultural Society and the Chelsea Flower Show may have taken a long time, but the results for both parties speak for themselves. **Be persistent and find creative ways to vary your pitch. If one approach doesn't work, try something else.**

It's time to learn how our contributors have used these approaches and ideas in their own practice.

The art of negotiating

I have worked with a number of senior IMG executives, and to my mind they remain true to Mark's legacy. They have a way of doing business, in terms of preparation and follow-up, which is consistent with Mark's writing, and consistent with top-class companies. There is also a negotiating style. I remember dealing with Barry Frank on negotiating rights to the college play-off system for ESPN. He understood how to get to 'yes': he made me make the first offer, and figured out how not to win everything but to let both parties win. We did a lot of business with Barry because of his approach, and I have had a similar experience with other executives.

I adhere to many of those principles myself. I agree that you should know what you want before you go into a deal. One of the things I say to my team before we go into a meeting is, what do we want to get out of this meeting, and what do we want the people who we are meeting to say to themselves once the meeting has finished and they are back out on the street?

I always want to be clear about what both parties want, so that we don't waste time and we know when to stop. One of the first things I try to achieve in a negotiation is for the other side to lay out what are their most important points – which may not always be about the figures. From my point of view, if I have five things I want, I ask for those five things. When I was head of content at ESPN, the role entailed negotiating a lot of deals. My predecessor's stance was to say 'no' unless there was a reason to say 'yes'. And he would use the 'no' to negotiate for concessions on other things. I took over and said we are going to say 'yes' unless there is a reason to say 'no'. We are not going to horse trade on things we are prepared to give anyway. Scorekeeping at a negotiation strikes me as a waste of time.

Being clear about what you want at the outset means that you can stop negotiating when you get them. Lots of people are reluctant to accept a 'yes' as they assume that if they had persevered, they could have got a better deal. If you stop when you have achieved what you hoped for at the outset, rather than trying to extract more, it is a fair result that will leave the other side feeling happy and positive towards you. People who say that they have won a negotiation amuse me. Unless you just want to do business with someone once, the only way to end a negotiation is with two happy parties.

Maybe some people enjoy the art of negotiation. I enjoy the result more than the process. I believe that that is the IMG way. If you tried to summarise the IMG way, it is a common-sense, philosophical method of getting results for your company and your clients. It chimes with my own principles, and I always enjoy doing business with them. I have never had an unfair process or result.

John Skipper

Focus on win-win

As I was learning about business, having never worked in another company before Playboy Enterprises and not having an MBA, I tended to concentrate on developing functional skills: finance, marketing, organisational development, which I did through academic programmes I attended and through exposure. I learned early the value of building a wide and deep network of advisers, and when I became president in 1982 and started to strengthen the Playboy Enterprises board of directors, Mark was one of the first people I asked to join.

I also learned from observing successful business people. I observed that most of the time, business was transactional. But not always. I saw in Mark a very different approach. Even though he was a consummate deal-maker, his style was to 'play the long game' by building a relationship first. I saw him do that through business entertaining, through getting to know, and keeping notes on, a person's interests and even their family, through looking for the small favours and courtesies that could be done and would be remembered. He deeply believed that people would much rather do business with someone they liked; and I believe that he was right. There is inestimable value in building a genuine relationship with the people with whom you want to do business.

He taught me to share of myself. I started appreciating the value in spending time understanding and exploring a new sales territory, rather than holing up in a hotel or conference room to hammer out deal points as soon as I arrived. When I became CEO and began growing Playboy Enterprises' international businesses, that learning was invaluable. I found that, particularly overseas, business people put a premium on getting to know you and wanted you to do the same. And the benefit wasn't just a greater likelihood of doing the deal in the first place, but a high degree of likelihood that if something unexpected occurred – whether an opportunity or a problem – the alignment and trust would be there to work it through.

Too often, people think of the art of negotiation as the ability to get what you want, when really it is the ability to understand the other sides' needs, wants, worries and desires in order to come together around a vision and structure that is a win-win. Mark was a master of that.

Christie Hefner

Bring passion to selling

To be able to persuade, you have to have a real knowledge and passion for your product. Mark and my boss John Beddington (who was ex-IMG) both had it, and IMG still does. Possessing that enthusiasm for your product, taking a more consultative sales approach to solve problems for the brand is one of the keys to IMG's enduring success.

When I am selling tennis, there is no question of my passion and how much I believe in the product. I am selling that belief. Quite often with sponsorship you are selling intangibles, how a player's brand is going to align around another brand. You have to have conviction to close a deal. You need to have the ability to convince your buyer that it is the right business solution for them and that you are going to be able to deliver. My commercial partners say that when I work with them I over-deliver. I act as if I am an employee of their brand and that is the way I think it has to be in order to close and sustain long-term sponsorship relationships.

The success of selling lies not in what you want to sell but understanding the buyer's position and working backwards. What's their business challenge? What is the opportunity or solution you can bring to them to grow their business? The other critical element is speed of execution once the deal has been agreed. I remember John getting on the phone to the lawyers straight after a meeting and saying we need this contract in 24 hours. After the first deal I made without John at Tennis Canada, I called the law firm and said exactly the same. Knowledge of, and belief in, your product, understanding your buyer's needs and following through with exceptional execution are the basic tenets of any successful sale.

Stacey Allaster

Understand the values involved in deals

Everything we did at Wimbledon was for the long term. Loyalty is part of our character and tradition, and it has a value. When we were renewing contracts, I would say to Mark that it was not worth talking to a potential new partner unless they were offering 20 per cent more. Unless a company was prepared to pay a serious premium, why would we change?

Wimbledon has a special character. It has a much longer lifespan than any of us, with more traditions, and it was important that the way we acted embodied the character of the brand. We say, 'players first, fans second, television last.' We would lose a lot of credibility if we chopped and changed all the time over small amounts of money. We needed to behave in a way that embodied Wimbledon values. Mark understood that and not only helped that process but also adopted it himself. I have kept two pieces of paper from my time with Mark. One is a £5 note from a bet that I won. The other is a piece of paper on which he wrote that *after* we had signed a television contract, I would tell him what his percentage would be. It was an extraordinary act, but showed our mutual understanding that when it came to negotiating, longevity was more important than incremental percentage rates. Understanding the values involved in deals will only help to cement relationships and lead to better outcomes for both parties.

John Curry

Set the scene

At one point, I was working with Mark on two completely separate projects. He called me into his meeting room to discuss a couple of issues on each one. The room was light and airy and had a lovely aspect overlooking the Thames in London. At one end of the room there was a sofa and armchair that looked out onto the river and made the most of the view. We started the meeting with him sitting on the sofa and me in an armchair sitting opposite him, both in relaxed mode.

We finished the discussion on the first topic, which was a personnel matter, and I was all for moving straight onto the next. Mark, however, cut me off immediately, saying, 'No, we have to move to the table now. This is a separate meeting and we want to discuss something completely different.' No one else had come into the room or altered the dynamic, but for Mark it was important that for the change to be made mentally, the scene be set differently.

Jean Cooke

SHORT SMART

Introduce yourself to everyone in the room. If there was the slightest chance that someone did not know him, Mark would introduce himself at the beginning of a meeting. He would not assume that they knew who he was because he was a big cheese. It put everyone at ease at the outset.

Buzz Hornett

Tone and context matter

Any negotiation will always go better if the other side are predisposed to think well of you. Setting a positive tone at the outset of a meeting is important, and something Mark understood very well.

Wimbledon had twice-yearly meetings with IMG and Mark often started proceedings with a cheque. This was quite often money that was due some months before, from completion of a licensing agreement perhaps, but he would choose to wait and give it to us personally. It's a rare client who will not react favourably to the presentation of a cheque for a six-figure sum.

He could adopt a more personal touch as well. Like Mark, I am a keen retainer of records, and I have a letter that he sent me in 2002, just a couple of days before we were due to meet. Enclosed were photos of his daughter Maggie, with the message, 'Since I know you are building a file for the 2013 wild cards in the women's singles, I thought you should add these pictures to it.' It's the kind of letter he would have sent me anyway, but sending it before we were due to meet was a nice touch.

We were not always on the receiving end of such treatment. We could also be part of it. When a television or other major deal was nearing completion, Mark tried to ensure that representatives from the AELTC would go out to the territory and meet with the key people. In Japan, for example, he suggested that we bring a team to play a couple of matches in and around Tokyo with some local clubs.

The involvement of the AELTC was always appreciated, and it gave Mark credibility to have the clients with him rather than just him negotiating on his own. It set the right tone. As a result, he secured a lot of goodwill that served IMG well when we needed to negotiate a new contract.

Chris Gorringe

Show respect for the world you're working in

When he was emerging as a global force, people gave Mark the nickname Mark the Shark. While many were impressed by his commercial acumen, there were some, including the United States Golf Association (USGA), that viewed his commercial success with suspicion. Mark invited members of the committee to his house for dinner one night. During the course of the evening, he showed them his most prized possessions, which he proudly had on display. They were his USGA medals from his days of playing as an amateur golfer. It transformed the relationship with USGA, who from then on did not look at him as if he was some sort of commercial juggernaut, about to ride roughshod over the game of golf in the name of commercialism. Instead they saw someone who loved and had huge respect for the game and was tremendously proud of the medals he had won. He was able to show that it is possible to be in the business of golf, without forgetting the spirit of the game, which revolves around integrity, fair play and an almost Corinthian spirit.

Since leaving IMG, I have worked in both golf and polo – the oldest team sport in the world – and my approach has always been to act with deep respect for the sport I am in. The business of a sport must complement its ethos, not undermine it. Getting the balance right between driving the sport commercially and retaining its spirit is fundamental to success.

Neil Hobday

Don't kill the golden goose

Mark got invited to speak at the Oxford Union, and although I was very junior at the time, I was an Oxford graduate and travelled there with him.

The speech itself went well and Mark handled a couple of tricky questions with some aplomb. Once the official part of the evening was over, he was greeted by Sir Roger Bannister, a don at Oxford, but immortalised for his four-minute mile. They talked for about half an hour and although I couldn't hear everything they said I thought it fascinating to see the man who modernised and commercialised sport deep in conversation with the doyen of amateur Corinthian sport. It was an intriguing juxtaposition between two worlds.

I went back in 2014, to hear a talk that Sir Roger was giving, 60 years to the day from when he ran his four-minute mile. I went up to him afterwards and explained that he probably wouldn't remember me but that I was there over twenty years ago with Mark McCormack. I was fascinated by his response. He said: 'Yes, I remember, I liked Mark very much. He really believed in the importance of sport itself. Although he could do clever things around it, he didn't want to do anything that would change the sanctity of the sporting endeavour, which in itself is the important thing.'

When we created the Indian Premier League (IPL) cricket league, someone suggested that if a player hit the ball to a certain spot, it should be rewarded with an eight rather than a six. But it was very quickly rejected because 'that's not cricket'. Mark transformed sport and the lives of all those connected with it, creating an industry where none existed before. But he knew better than to mess with the essence and the magic of sport itself. He knew what was important and respected that.

Guy Kinnings

SHORT SMART

Be aware of, and respect, dress codes. I always wear a tie when I am at The All England [Lawn Tennis] Club during The Championships. It is a private members' club and the members are in ties and jackets. I feel like I'm a guest and need to show respect, even though I have credentials that will get me almost anywhere. It is something I noticed in, and copied from, Mark, who always wore a tie to the Club and always looked professional, which is important.

Tony Godsick

Understand your own strength

In 1983, Australia won the America's Cup for the Royal Perth Yacht Club. It was a big deal, with the win ending a 132-year tenure by the New York Yacht Club. It also meant that for the first time in over a century, the America's Cup Challenge would move from New York to Perth, as the rules stipulate that the winners host the next competition. We were representing Alan Bond, the owner of the winning yacht, and Perth, in their defence of the Cup. An organising committee had been set up to deal with the multitude of rules and regulations surrounding the event, but progress was painfully slow. Having held the title and therefore been in control for so long, the New York Yacht Club were trying to dominate proceedings. They were affecting an air of superiority in an attempt to dictate their terms.

Mark saw what was going on and took the Perth committee aside. He said, 'Just tell them they're not invited. It's your game, your rules. You won, so you decide. Just don't invite them.'

After they had got over the shock of what Mark was suggesting it was as if a massive light bulb had gone off in the room. It was a lovely moment, to watch this dawning realisation of the power they had. Before that, the Royal Perth Yacht Club had seen the New York Yacht Club as the more prestigious club that needed to be shown respect. Suddenly, they saw themselves as equals, and rightly so as they had ownership of the Cup. In the event, such radical action was not necessary but, confronted with this newly found confidence, the Americans backed down on whatever rules and regulations they had been trying to fix in their favour. It showed the importance of looking beyond appearances and bluster, and of assessing who has the real position of strength in a negotiation.

Ian Todd

Find the gatekeeper and success will follow

As a good amateur player himself, Mark was passionately keen on golf and the Open in particular. The Open was run by the

Royal and Ancient Golf Club (R&A), which back in the seventies was nearly broke. It was obvious that they couldn't put up the necessary prize money to keep the Open on a par with the other majors. Most people were saying that in five years' time it would no longer be running. Mark, however, was desperate for it to succeed, and so it was hugely important to him that he got on side with the R&A. It so happened that I was the key to the gate.

Mark had been speaking to the secretary of the R&A, but the two did not get on. Our secretary at the time didn't see any need for Mark and was strongly against the appointment of an outfit like IMG. But I couldn't sit by and watch the oldest championship in the world disappear.

When I became chairman, the Championship Committee was the most powerful committee at St Andrews, slightly more so than the General Committee. I had been included in the conversations about Mark's involvement and I was hugely enthusiastic about it. I knew that involving Mark would be the way to get the money the Club needed. Wimbledon had already employed Mark and my investigations showed that they were delighted with his work. I reported back to the Championship Committee and was given the authority to do the negotiations with Mark. The General Committee however, were not impressed and the chairman resigned on principle, proclaiming that the R&A should not be commercialised.

Despite the antipathy from some, once Mark was on board his appointment proved to be an instant success. I went to New York with him to renew the television contract we had, and I was slack-jawed listening to the negotiations. At that time we were getting $100k from ABC for US broadcasting rights. We went in to see ABC and Mark said we should tear up the existing agreement, and start at one, with a view to moving up to five in three years. I then realised that he was talking about one million, and my mouth almost hit the floor.

He hadn't discussed numbers with me beforehand and I was very worried. I felt obliged to say to ABC that, while I was obviously interested in raising the fee, I was more interested in not having the name of the Club sullied in any way. I didn't want there to be an adverse reaction to the contract or any resentment. I felt it was such a huge change. But Mark was proved right and they agreed with no quibble.

Afterwards I asked Mark how on earth he had come up with those figures. He had found out how much ABC intended to get from their advertising rights, and he was looking for a fair distribution of that revenue. It wasn't a random figure plucked out of the air. IMG then got the marketing rights and Mark negotiated television contracts in Japan, Australia and Spain. The R&A grew far stronger as a result.

We had a strong relationship and became good friends. I had confidence in what he was recommending and he sought my advice on internal R&A matters. He understood that involvement with an institution such as the R&A wouldn't be easy, but he was confident in what he was recommending and that I could help smooth the path. I, in turn, was rightly confident that he would deliver.

Colin Maclaine

Don't put all your eggs in one basket

When Christopher Skase bought Channel 7, a major Australian television network, one of his top priorities was to get into sports in a big way. He had a big ego, and was ready to spend lots of money. Unsurprisingly, and with little trouble at all, my father persuaded him to buy a number of golf events for multiples of what anyone had ever paid before.

What struck me as I watched the negotiations unfold was that my father was clearly hoping to protect a few key events for the incumbent broadcaster, Kerry Packer's Channel 9, which had previously held the rights to most of the golf events. His dilemma was this. On the one hand, an agent has a fiduciary obligation to get the best price for each of his clients. On the other hand, we did numerous deals with each of the major networks, and it was important to have a good relationship with all of them. My father navigated these tricky waters by making sure that all parties felt like they were treated fairly and got most of what they wanted, even if they could not have it all. He explained to Skase that it would be difficult or impossible to get the rights to the events that would probably remain with Channel 9, but that the events they did get would be enough to make Channel 7 the dominant golf network. He then explained to Channel 9 that they had been blown out of the water on certain golf events by Channel 7, but there was a chance to step up to the mark on the remaining events. Since Channel 7 was waiting in the wings, they promptly did so.

In the end, all of the golf events saw huge increases in rights fees and exposure. And, importantly, there were now two parties ready to bid for future events and two parties ready and willing to heavily promote the sport of golf. This was an important lesson in not putting all of our eggs in one basket.

Breck McCormack

Don't take no for an answer

I remember Mark coming back from the US and talking about Brian Roggenburk, an executive in Cleveland. Brian had got hold of a disparate group of people who ran home and garden shows in Philadelphia, Seattle and Chicago. He organised them and secured sponsorship. Mark was clearly impressed and asked me, 'Why don't we do that in the UK? What is there?' I replied that we have the Hampton Court Show and the Chelsea Flower Show and that's about it. His immediate response was, 'Well, we should be helping them.'

So for four years we knocked on the door of the Royal Horticultural Society (RHS). At first, they were very unreceptive to the idea. The chairman explained that the members felt insecure about IMG's involvement. They had a natural aversion to what we did, and were nervous about what we might suggest and how that might affect their reputation. We explained that there was no need for insecurity, and stressed that the commercial benefits for the RHS could be achieved without damaging their image.

Mark would ask me from time to time how we were progressing with the relationship, to which the reply was not very far. He finally came to a meeting to explain to the RHS that it wasn't a terrible thing to do to get sponsorship for a royal event. He pointed to Wimbledon and the AELTC and our ability to work with people who were equally nervous about the idea of sponsorship. Things continued in this vein for four years, until eventually, and purely as a result of Mark's persistence, the RHS saw the light.

The first major sponsorship represented a significant amount of money for the RHS, which allowed them to embark on a multimillion-pound project to digitise the biggest horticultural library on the planet, at Vincent Square in London. We introduced them to hospitality at the Chelsea Flower Show, and the very popular breakfast show, where people gain early access to the show, enjoy breakfast and see everything before the doors open to the public. Not giving up on what sometimes seemed a hopeless negotiation eventually bore fruit. We gained a valuable new client and the RHS gained new revenue streams that helped them to expand their activity and influence.

Jeremy Palmer-Tomkinson

Be honest and open

In the early 1990s the Royal Canadian Golf Association (RCGA) faced a challenge that threatened the future of the Canadian Open Championship. Government legislation prohibiting cigarette companies from sponsoring sporting events was about to be enacted. Up until 1992, the Open received 90 per cent of its funding from Imperial Tobacco. The loss of this income would doom the tournament.

We felt that the correct approach was to convince Imperial Tobacco that for the good of the sport, and to protect the legacy they had helped create, they should loosen control of the branding of the event, while continuing to fund it, and allow us to introduce prospective replacements gradually. We reasoned that this would improve the possibility of securing a new title sponsor within three years. We proposed that IMG be retained to execute this strategy.

The problem was that, as managing director of IMG Canada, I would be leading the charge but I had never really played golf, despite it being a cornerstone of IMG's success. To overcome this, I asked Mark to request a meeting with the board of the RCGA and our consulting team, a meeting that Mark would join personally. The RCGA accepted.

During the meeting, we leaned heavily on Mark's global credibility, and we backed that up with data, research and a well thought-out strategy to solve their dilemma. Towards the end, and in spite of our efforts, the chairman of the RCGA board, an avid, lifelong golfer, studied me and asked: 'Michael, why should we entrust the future of the Open to a group led by someone who does not even play golf?'

Mark allowed me to reply, and rather than trying to dredge up some connection with golf or some hitherto hidden interest in the sport, I said, 'John, you've been to our performances of Stars on Ice many times.' He nodded and smiled. 'I'm sure it won't surprise you that although I played quite a bit of ice hockey, I can't land a triple axel or carve a figure eight onto an ice surface … and yet we operate the most successful figure-skating tour in Canada's history.' And I left it there.

We began working for the RCGA the next month and IMG Canada has had a relationship with the Open ever since.

Five years later when I was recruiting NASCAR racing

champion Jeff Gordon, I found myself in a similar situation. We had convinced Jeff to consider signing with IMG as our marquee client in the new Charlotte, North Carolina Motorsports practice. As the meeting in Daytona was drawing to an end and a representation agreement was imminent, I told Jeff, 'I'm looking forward to seeing my first NASCAR race tomorrow.'

'You mean your first Daytona 500?' he corrected.

'No, my first race anywhere,' I replied.

He smiled and later admitted that one of the reasons he had decided to proceed was that anyone who would admit that he had never attended a race, before signing a race-car driver, would have to be a pretty honest guy. Once again, honesty had proved to be the best policy.

Michael Wright

Selling is a life skill

In my early days, when I first read *What They Don't Teach You at Harvard Business School*, I had a meeting with Elliott Kerr who was then president of IMG Canada. I remember him telling me that people who can run events, or can do marketing, are a dime a dozen, but that there are very few who know how to sell. Those that know how to make money, save money or make the brand look good will be successful. Mark talked about the power of persuasion. You may not necessarily be selling sponsorship or an athlete, but ultimately you are always selling yourself – your ideas and your strategies. You are inspiring other people to follow, and to do that, you need to know how to sell, how to persuade, in order to achieve your personal and professional goals.

Whenever young industry colleagues come and ask me for advice, that's the number one thing that I say to them. I advise them to go and work in the front office, sell tickets and understand customers. Know what it is like to be on the front line. It is critical. I was not a born salesperson, and was uncomfortable with it. Still to this day it's not my natural tendency, but you have to learn how to do it. Even if you never sell a widget or a sponsorship, you have to know how to sell yourself and your ideas. It is a life skill.

I think for women in particular it is critical. As they climb up the ladder, it becomes more and more intimidating for them, and I am shocked by the number of women who don't have the same self-confidence to put themselves forward as men do. That's exactly when the life skill of selling comes into its own.

Stacey Allaster

5

Making it happen

*The art of selling is the conscious practice of a lot
of things we already know unconsciously ...*

So, you've done your homework and arrived at a negotiating approach that'll work for you. Now you have to make it happen. This chapter gives you some practical common-sense strategies to help you succeed. Here you'll find examples of classic negotiating techniques such as under-promising and over-delivering, how to overcome objections, and when you'll need to hold your nerve.

The NFL's Peter Griffiths opens with a great example of positioning, with a potentially confrontational meeting turned on its head by refocusing the discussion onto developing rather than revisiting a relationship – extending that classic win-win we're all looking for. It's almost always advantageous to **control the agenda** in this way. The classic MHM tip of being proactive and scheduling phone calls rather than being on the receiving end is another way of taking the initiative, a technique used to good advantage by Leslie McCormack Gathy.

MHM's advocacy of **'just showing up' can also lead to a breakthrough**, as USA Rugby's Bob Latham demonstrates; his courting of key decision makers helped to sway the IOC vote to include rugby sevens in the 2016 Olympic Games. Sometimes, you just need to be there for a face-to-face meeting.

It's always tricky to place a value on what you're selling. **Taking**

price out of the equation can be a powerful strategy for getting the deal done. Peter Dawson and Ian Todd both show the value of the principle of never making an offer and of putting the other party on the spot. MHM's son, Breck McCormack, remembers that his father often suggested that the other party should pay what they considered the deal was worth – which could end up being nothing. But by removing any resistance based on price, the dynamic of the negotiation changed, and both parties were able to concentrate on the true merits (or otherwise) of what was being discussed.

The numbers should never be the only focus of a negotiation, and there will be many other factors at play based on what you're offering, your negotiating partner, and the circumstances surrounding the deal. Two things are clear, though. First, **selling yourself and your product short will only undermine your position.** If you are confident about what you're offering, you should hold your nerve, as Gavin Forbes illustrates. On the other hand, **don't overprice just because you can.** Greed is never attractive and will undoubtedly damage the potential for long-term collaboration.

Two chapters of *What They Don't Teach You ...* are devoted to the power of silence and the importance of timing in selling and negotiation, and both themes are picked up by the *Beyond Harvard* contributors. Most people feel uncomfortable with silence and the tendency is to speak to fill the vacuum. MHM strongly advised against this, advocating the strategic use of silence as an important negotiating tool. As Jeremy Palmer-Tomkinson reminds us, **you learn by listening rather than speaking.** A silence allows the other person to talk and will often force them to divulge something that gives you an edge. And when the deal is done or the message delivered, keep your counsel and move on.

Any negotiation also has to take account of timing and patience. **'Read the mood'; make a judgement call on when the time is right to make a pitch.** Even seasoned professionals like

MHM could get it wrong. Tim Sullivan, former president of The College of William and Mary, tells us about MHM's ill-timed and ill-fated encounter with Margaret Thatcher at a College reception. Leslie McCormack Gathy's account of IMG's developing relationship with Sara Lee shows **the power of patience in long-term deal making**. People and events often move at their own pace and you may need to adjust your timing to fall into step.

There is much to learn from the strategies that follow.

Know how to avoid conflict

In one of my first meetings with Mark, I was given a masterclass in how to defuse a potentially confrontational situation. The meeting was with an important client, a sports federation. We had a long-term contract with the federation to represent their sponsorship rights. In order to win the rights we had bid quite high, and had lost money in the first few years. Then, suddenly, interest in their sport exploded. We were recouping what we had lost and things were looking rosy. The federation however, thought that this increased interest now made the contract unfair and called a meeting to discuss its terms.

At first, it was the classic confrontational seating plan, with us on one side of the table and the clients on the other. Then Mark joined the meeting and sat at the head of the table. It was brilliant body language. He had teed himself up as being the arbiter between two factions, rather than sitting with us.

He then took control and divided up his opening comments into three phases. First, he flattered, saying how good a client they were and how we valued the relationship with them and wanted to make the sport and their rights stronger for our mutual benefit. Then he paused, and said that this scenario was similar to them selling their house. When they sold it, we had agreed a price that at the time we all thought was fair. It didn't seem correct for them to come back now and say that they wanted more money because the value of the house had gone up. In the same way, it wouldn't seem correct if it had gone down in value, and we had come back to them saying we wanted to pay less.

With the point made, he then went on to say that we understood their issues, but maybe we should think about what more we should be doing to help them. Rather than fighting over this one contract, what other things could we be doing? Could we be representing them in other areas to generate more revenue for them?

Mark had flattered, scolded and then searched for a mutual solution. We never got into the fight over the contract. It became a joint search for things we could do, and the meeting ended on a positive note. The way that Mark positioned himself turned what could have been an aggressive meeting into a mutual gain.

Peter Griffiths

Book a call to break through

Growing up, we always knew when my dad was going to call home, as it had been scheduled in. He'd prepare his 'Talk to Leslie' list in advance (on the appropriate 3 × 5 index cards) and you could figuratively and literally hear him ticking items off his list as the conversation unfurled. There was little time for spontaneous chit-chat. Phone calls were not only scheduled for a specific time, they also had a scheduled end – at least in his mind. He (or his assistant) planned his calls in advance and he would always ring you. My dad had long before determined that it's much easier to have your thoughts together, to control the call's agenda and to keep an eye on your schedule for the entire day if you instigate the call.

This led to large amounts of amusement and frustration on my part, particularly as a young girl, when calls were inevitably shorter than I would have hoped. Even as an adult, I remember once calling him for his birthday – in between two meetings and a flight of my own – only to be told he wasn't free to speak!

Nevertheless, the idea of scheduling a phone call always stuck with me, and certainly proved its worth in one negotiation.

In 2003, IMG was up against several agencies to win the right to implement General Electric's first-ever worldwide Olympic sponsorship agreement. One of GE's major assets, the broadcaster NBC, was arguably one of the most important and influential players in the Olympic Movement. However, GE would need the help of an experienced agency to help them develop a creative marketing plan that allowed them to hit the ground running in Greece.

More than eager to get the business, IMG threw a huge amount of financial resources and experienced personnel into our pitch. Over many months, the team traversed the Atlantic to prepare, pitch and present to GE's marketing team. We made good progress but despite the positive feedback, GE continued to drag its feet.

With our negotiations stalled and a serious annual consulting fee in the offing, I decided to apply a McCormack street smart I knew very well. While attending the World Sports Forum together in 2002 in Lausanne, my dad had introduced me to Dick Ebersol, chairman of NBC Sports & Olympics. Critically, as GE owned NBC, it looked to the broadcaster for guidance on all things Olympics. I took a punt that Dick would remember me from our one brief meeting the year before. I called his assistant and arranged a time to speak to him. When I called his office at the appointed hour on the appointed day, Dick didn't even say hello. Rather, he greeted me with: 'The only other person in the whole world who ever booked a phone call with me was your father. How can I help you?' I briefly summarised our situation with GE, explained how important the GE business was to us and simply asked if he could put in a good word for IMG. Our call lasted maybe three 'McCormack minutes' but thanks to the call, we got the deal and our first worldwide Olympic Consulting client. Treating an important phone call with the pre-planning and respect it deserved made all the difference.

Leslie McCormack Gathy

Negotiate with whoever has the power

Very often, the people I negotiated with would want to meet my boss because, after all, he was the one signing the cheque. I might be negotiating for HBO to televise a prize fight, but ultimately HBO was not my company and it was not my money. I just had a budget. Some people took the view that, if a deal is worth millions of dollars, they wanted to meet the top dog. That was never the case with Mark. He was shrewd enough to know that my chairman would support me in whatever steps I took to secure the Wimbledon contract, and he had no need to have his ego massaged by meeting my boss who would just reinforce the stance I had already taken. In fact, it would be a waste of his time, a commodity that he measured very carefully. Mark assumed that I was representing HBO and if I said HBO would pay X, then HBO would pay X and would honour the deal. I respected him hugely for that. He trusted what I said, which made negotiations for Wimbledon rights very straightforward and pretty simple.

Seth Abraham

The power of showing up

One sub-chapter of *What They Don't Teach You at Harvard Business School* that resonated with me over the years is entitled 'Show Up'. Woody Allen once said that, '80 per cent of success is just showing up.' Mark may not have put the percentage quite that high, but he wrote about the value of in-person meetings.

For many years I was involved in the effort to get rugby sevens into the Olympics. It was a more challenging sell in parts of the world without a long rugby tradition, one of those being Latin America. For a long time, we tried to get an audience with Mario Vazquez Rana, the president of the Pan American Sports Organization (PASO), based in Mexico City, and a leading Olympic figure. We wanted support for the inclusion of rugby in the Pan Am Games, as an initial step towards rugby as an Olympic sport. It took about a year for us to break through, but, one day, we were given about a week's notice that he would be available the following Monday. Five of us from various parts of the world descended upon Mexico City. Was it inconvenient? Yes. Was it critical? Yes. It was a very cordial meeting, with Vazquez Rana asking questions and giving us more time than allocated (not to mention a bottle of his own private reserve tequila). And it gave a great boost to our effort.

As a result, Vazquez Rana expedited our admission into the Pan Am Games and we were fast-tracked into the Central American and Caribbean Games. Just as important, the National Olympic Committees of other Latin American countries, such as the Dominican Republic and Cuba, began to take an interest in rugby. Showing up in Mexico City created that momentum, as did showing up in other parts of the world where the mission wasn't particularly specific, other than to try to forge relationships and advocate to any audience we could find. When the IOC voted in 2009 on which sports would be added to the 2016 Olympics, the vote was 81–8 in favour of the admission of rugby sevens.

Bob Latham

Put the other party on the spot

When I took up my post at the R&A, one of the first things I wanted to sort out were the commission rates we were paying to IMG. We had different rates depending on the type of work or the geographical area in which it was conducted, and this sometimes led to conflict. I raised the issue with Mark, and instead of justifying the position or suggesting a rate, he said, 'OK, you just tell me what you think is fair.'

It was a very clever move. He guessed that I wouldn't come up with something ridiculous and also knew that he would have a more satisfied client. It was a win-win. He said the same thing every time I questioned the financial arrangements between us. He would put the onus back onto me, so that I would have to come up with a proposal that made sense for both parties. It got to the point where I would just say, 'Shall I let you know what I think is fair, Mark?!'

This faith that I would come up with a sensible and fair arrangement was reinforced by the fact that at that time there were no formal written contracts between the R&A and IMG. We could have walked away from IMG at any point with no notice, but our relationship was such that that would have been inconceivable.

Peter Dawson

Ask for an offer

Mark's approach to negotiations was to get people to make an offer. If we had a new young tennis-playing client, we would go to say, Nike, and ask them to make an offer for the player to endorse their products. The whole objective was to get them to put a number on the table, which we could use as a base when approaching the next company. We would then go to Reebok and ask them to come up with an offer that bettered the one we already had. If all went to plan, we could go back to Nike with Reebok's higher offer, and ask them to up their initial bid. It was a tactic that worked very well.

When I left IMG and went to Nike, I told them not to play the game. I instructed them to ask the player's agent how much they wanted, and not to put an offer down. IMG should come up with a figure that we would either accept or reject, and they would not hear a number from us.

It wasn't long before I had a call from Mark. 'Ian,' he said, 'you have got our lot completely confused!'

Ian Todd

Take price out of the equation

One tactic that people remember my father for was telling the person with whom he was negotiating to take what we were offering and then pay us later what they thought it was worth. He would tell them that they could even pay nothing at all if they liked.

Funnily enough, I can't recall any cases where people took him up on this offer, but if this tactic didn't impact on the closing of the sale, it definitely changed the dynamic of the discussion. Any resistance based on price was instantly removed. It helped everyone agree about whether the opportunity being discussed was of genuine interest and we were negotiating over the price, or whether it really wasn't of interest at any price. If an idea is not of interest no matter how low the price, then it is time to move on and focus on something else that might work better for all parties.

Breck McCormack

Don't sell short

Quite early on in my career at IMG I was managing Pete Sampras. He was a young player but was clearly going to be very, very good. Pete had an adviser who could clearly see this too, and kept plugging away, pointing out that other agencies were prepared to offer a much lower commission rate, and that he, Pete, should start looking after number one. Pete duly approached me suggesting that we offer a commission rate that at the time was lower than that offered to our players ranked number one in the world. I called up Mark and Bob Kain who was one of Mark's top men, who both said that's not the way we do business. Mark's analogy was that if you buy a Mercedes you expect to pay more than if you buy a Ford, because you are buying a better quality product. He saw IMG as the Mercedes of management. We had a network of offices and a global infrastructure that was unrivalled and we could provide the best commercial and personal service for clients. That combined with the events management and television coverage meant that the amount of money a client would make net of commission would be more than they could receive by signing with any of our competitors who had a tenth of the resources around the world.

I explained Mark's rationale to Pete, but he was unconvinced and left me for the outfit that offered the lower commission. I was very upset by it, thinking we had lost a golden opportunity. It can be devastating to lose a client, and something that you take personally. Shortly after that he won the US Open, and all I could think was, 'wow, this is what it could have been.'

But Mark told me not to worry about it and that things would work out. He was really supportive, reiterating that I should take a long-term view and that it would all come good in the end. Sure enough, after a few months Pete called me admitting that he had made a mistake and that things hadn't worked out how he thought they would. At the end of his three-year contract with the other agency, he came back on similar terms and by then he was top of the world. If your product is good enough and you have belief in it, there is no need to sell yourself short.

Gavin Forbes

Never overprice just because you can

When you enter a negotiation with someone, do not do it on the fly. Rehearse each element of the presentation, have all the facts at your fingertips, and decide in advance what is a good price. And a good price is not the top dollar. The buyer must be able to walk away from the table feeling happy about the agreement.

Steffi Graf and Boris Becker were attracting huge interest in tennis in Germany at the same time as a new pay TV channel was starting. The European television rights to Wimbledon were held by the EBU, a collective of mainly government-owned, public service broadcasters. Mark sensed that the Club was ready for change. It was going to be a huge decision for Wimbledon. His preferred alternative for buying the European rights was the German-based Bertelsmann Media Group (BMG), who were very keen to be involved and to maximise the potential of the Graf/Becker effect and their new TV channel.

Mark got BMG to make a potential bid to the Club that represented a big increase, but was also a fair reflection of the increased interest within Germany. Prior to the final meeting with the Club committee, Mark had teed everyone up in pre-meetings that the Club should go with BMG and had rehearsed accordingly. When it came to the final meeting, the AELTC sat on one side, BMG on the other but the people from IMG were sprinkled among them so that we didn't appear to be taking sides. He had primed us all to contribute our bits beforehand. He barely spoke in order to ensure his impartiality. It made him merely a moderator.

On the back of that successful deal, BMG definitely became a friend. They knew that they wouldn't even have been at the Wimbledon table without Mark's assistance. Riding the wave of the Graf/Becker era, the Club was happy because it received a four-fold increase on the TV rights for Europe. In turn, BMG were satisfied that they had paid a fair price but not an over-inflated one that could have been forced upon them. As a result, they became buyers across a range of products, even as Graf and Becker retired and BMG's interest in Wimbledon waned. We had a thousand different products in our catalogue, which they would neither have known about nor wanted to know about had dealing with us over Wimbledon not been a pleasant experience.

It was Mark's view that if people believe that they have bought at a fair price, they become friends who like doing business with you time and again. If they feel that they have overpaid, the next time round they could make life very difficult. With BMG, and with numerous other examples, this proved to be correct.

Buzz Hornett

Under-promise and over-deliver

When you are sitting in front of a client or potential client, the temptation is to agree that you can do anything they suggest. Mark would always counsel against that approach. Without doubt it is better to make sure that what you offer you can deliver. In that way you stand a greater chance of developing a long-term relationship, and the benefits that flow from that understanding, rather than losing them and having to go through the exercise of replacing them.

It's tougher in a more competitive world, but probably even more relevant. Now there are a huge number of agencies, and a lot of the aspirational new ones will do anything to get that business. You somehow have to find the balance between not playing down your own offering so much that they go with the false prophet, but equally not promising what is ridiculous. The way that we have built long-term relationships with the R&A, European Tour, Wimbledon and Rolex, is by doing what we say we'll do and not over-promising. We work very closely with HSBC and have done for many years. It is rare for brands to stay as involved for so long with different projects. They will only do that if you are delivering, and you can only deliver if you set realistic expectations.

Guy Kinnings

Play the experience card

As IMG grew, a constant criticism levelled at us was that we could not act in our clients' best interests as we had too many conflicts of interest. There were too many instances when we acted for both parties trying to negotiate a deal, or we were too big and had our fingers in too many pies. Prospective clients would say that they would be better off going to a smaller agency who could focus purely on their interests.

The response to that, which I heard from others and adopted myself, was to play the experience card. I would say that, if you have a heart problem and you are concerned about it, you might travel around with a cardiologist who can monitor your heart rate and provide new prescriptions and medicine and run regular check-ups. That is one thing. But as soon as you discover you need surgery to whom are you going to turn? Not that person, but a surgeon with a lot of experience in conducting surgery, someone you feel safe with and who has a proven track record. That was a powerful analogy that made a difference. If you have the right experience, you should use it to your competitive advantage.

Alastair Johnston

The power of silence

One of the things that I took from *What They Don't Teach You at Harvard Business School* was the power of silence in a negotiation. It is now the first thing that comes into my head when I approach a negotiation with a client, an athlete or even with my staff. My natural tendency is to be uncomfortable with silence in the room. A lot of people feel the same, and end up saying something to be nice or to fill the void, which then detracts from the point they are trying to make. It also means that they can give themselves away and start conceding points before they are ready to do so.

I have started to appreciate the value of silence in different scenarios. I once had to have a difficult conversation about a demotion with someone who reported to me. I made my points and finished the discussion. Her first comment back to me was that I had handled the conversation very well. When I asked her why she thought that, she said, 'You were very direct, you gave your examples as to what has brought us to this situation, and then you stopped talking.'

No one wants to have the conversation I had with that employee. The tendency is to try to soften the blow by talking through awkward silences. But by doing so, the actual point you are making gets lost and the person you are talking to doesn't understand what you are saying. That can make the conversation even more awkward and protracted. Be direct and then stop talking – the other person will appreciate it.

Zaileen Janmohamed

You learn through listening not speaking

No one likes a loud mouth, even if the loud mouth deserves to have the loudest mouth on the planet, which in many instances you could say Mark did. If you come into a meeting full of bombast, it naturally creates barriers between you and the people you want to work with. If you listen, you get so much further in business. Mark honed that to perfection. He would give himself the best possible chance of assessing a meeting or the clients in it by giving himself time to read every situation.

It started with his understated air. Mark was styleless. He didn't want any flamboyance or style attached to him that would detract from the clients. He wasn't someone who wanted or needed to be seen to be a huge success and was not into any pomp or ceremony. He always dressed the same way, very conservatively and middle-of-the-road. He didn't want the attention on him, just on what he was saying – when the time came to speak.

Jeremy Palmer-Tomkinson

Disarming one-liners and how to use them

George Blumberg, a successful businessman from South Africa, was the person who introduced my father to Gary Player in the 1960s. One night, he and his wife Brenda joined our family for a dinner in Paris with a prominent European businessman who my father was intent on doing business with. Although he was a larger-than-life character, George was quieter than usual while our dinner guest dominated the conversation. Given the prospect of potential business for IMG, my father laughed at his jokes dutifully and encouraged him with his questions, while the guest never once reciprocated by asking anyone else at the table a question.

As dinner ended, we made our way to the kerb, taxis were hailed and we said our goodbyes. Before our guest jumped in his cab he went over to George and said, 'Goodnight. It was nice talking with you.' George delivered his response without blinking an eye. 'Yes, it was nice listening to you.'

It was the first sentence George had uttered in an hour. It clearly made its mark, as, for the first time that evening, our European guest was lost for words. I remembered talking about this with my dad afterwards, and there were two lessons I learned from this incident. First, you need to understand the relationship dynamics within every situation; you must never lose your core integrity and good manners. Second, a well-crafted sentence can have more impact than an extended rant or monologue. Decades later, I don't remember one thing our guest said that night but I've never forgotten George's perfect retort on that street corner in Paris.

Todd McCormack

How to overcome objections

During my presidency at the College of William and Mary, Mark (an alumnus) chaired the campaign to raise $153m, which was a significant sum and a very important step in our development. At one point, we were raising funds for athletic facilities and dealing with a particularly difficult donor who didn't have much interest in doing what we wanted him to do.

Mark asked us to set up a meeting with the donor, and then insisted on being briefed in minute detail, and on explaining why this particular gift would be important to him. At the meeting itself, he listened attentively to what the donor was saying, and within a relatively short space of time, Mark had uncovered the roots of his concern, and what might be standing in his way. By listening and tuning in to what people were saying, Mark was able to derive insights into their personalities and use these to get the best possible result. The donor gave Mark a list of two or three concerns. In reply, Mark said: 'I'm going to write down these concerns and I will have someone get in touch with you directly.' He also pointed out that he had himself made a multimillion-dollar commitment to the College's McCormack-Nagelsen tennis facility, which gave the donor confidence that his concerns would be addressed.

The very next day Mark's associate called and talked through the issues, and the day after that Mark followed up. He was relentless. And it paid off. A combination of research, listening hard, speed of response, and leading by example meant that he got to 'yes' and the deal was done.

Tim Sullivan

Hold your nerve

When Mark first started working with Wimbledon and the R&A, there was no television money in Europe. Rights were negotiated through the European Broadcast Union (EBU), who paid a fraction of the sum that NBC paid in the US. To my amazement, Mark told me that we were going to guarantee Wimbledon a significant increase from the EBU for the rights to the next Championships. The EBU asked for a meeting with us during the French Open at Roland Garros – just one month before Wimbledon. I don't think I have ever seen Mark as nervous as he then was, but there was a determined look in his eye. He felt that the EBU was using its dominant position to threaten never to buy TV rights from IMG again should Wimbledon not come at a price they were happy with. In the days before Sky and other broadcasters had entered the arena, the EBU was a cartel that believed they had the power to name their price.

We walked into the room to be confronted by twelve stony-faced men, representatives from each of the major EBU countries. Mark looked at them and spoke very plainly. He said: 'I don't like being threatened. You will no doubt survive perfectly well without buying rights from us. We will probably struggle to survive as well or grow if you don't buy rights from us, but there is no way I am being threatened.' The meeting lasted about two minutes.

The second attempt, less than two weeks later, was in New York and was equally short. The EBU flew out for a meeting at the IMG offices. It was a rainy day and they had just managed to take their raincoats off and order tea and coffee when Mark asked them to leave, disgusted at what he viewed as a ludicrously low offer.

On the one hand, Mark had Wimbledon, for whom the idea of not having European television coverage would be devastating. On the other hand, he had the EBU, in theory one of IMG's biggest clients. Had the deal not come off, it would have been incredibly damaging. However, Mark felt so strongly that the EBU were taking advantage of the situation that he was prepared to lay everything on the line. He had the courage of his convictions and believed that the EBU would have to come round. And they did. We finally did the deal with the EBU on the eve of The Championships. It was fascinating to watch and an insight into the power of holding your nerve.

Ian Todd

Get your timing right

For a business deal to take off, the timing has to be right for both parties. Unfortunately, this was not always the case with Mark, when his enthusiasm could sometimes get the better of him.

Lady Thatcher was, for seven years, chancellor of The College of William and Mary. It is an honorary position, and involves representing the College at important meetings and hosting receptions at which we could promote the image of the university to important and influential people. We were hosting one such reception in Lady Thatcher's honour at the IMG office in New York, which was a magnificent nineteenth-century town house.

The idea was that she would speak and then be at the centre of the event, being introduced to various people. Mark said to me that he would like some private time with her. I asked him what for, but he just repeated the request, so we went ahead and arranged it.

The reception came, and at the allotted time, the two disappeared into a room together. When Lady Thatcher emerged, I could see in her eyes that something had surprised her. She said to me: 'That man is amazing. He wanted to make a business deal with me,' before adding, 'but I didn't think I was ready.' She was a combination of bemused and amused that a man she had not met before had tried to do a deal with her right in the middle of her reception.

Tim Sullivan

Don't make them run before they can walk

One of my dad's enduring lessons was to be patient. When you are building a relationship, understand that sometimes it's OK not to rush in with the big deal, even if you can see the benefits to all parties. Being patient and starting with baby steps can ultimately get you much further.

In the mid-1990s IMG signed Justine Henin, a young tennis player from Belgium. Around the same time, we were introduced to Frank Meysman, the chair of Sara Lee Europe. An inveterate tennis fan, Frank found the prospect of getting involved with women's tennis enticing. A large number of Sara Lee's food and household products appealed to women and he immediately saw the enormous potential.

Although Sara Lee was a multinational corporation with deep pockets, it was clear that to rush in with the easy but expensive option of endorsing the world number one player, Martina Hingis, would be the wrong first step. Instead, Frank, a fellow Belgian, agreed that Sara Lee would underwrite Justine's annual budget, providing her with much-needed financial support. The gamble paid off. At barely fifteen and wearing the Sara Lee patches for the first time, Justine won the Roland Garros Junior Girls event in 1997.

As the IMG/Sara Lee relationship grew, Frank became increasingly enamoured with women's tennis. He recognised how the Women's Tennis Association (WTA) Tour, and its personalities, could help him widen brand recognition of the little-known Sanex line of body-care products. Following Justine's success in Paris, the Henin deal was replicated with other players to create the Sanex Team.

Next, IMG secured the sanction to a lower-tier tournament on the WTA Tour and ran it in Belgium. Although a lower-level event, we made the Sanex Trophy feel as important as a Grand

Slam. Corporately, the tournament was a showcase of all that Sara Lee represented. Sanex was the title sponsor but IMG found ways to also promote other Sara Lee brands.

This was the time to take the big step. IMG represented the WTA for many years and was working to sell its title sponsorship. We had thought for some time that Sara Lee/Sanex were an obvious fit, but despite his enthusiasm, trying to make Frank jump into a multimillion-dollar sponsorship of the WTA Tour at the outset would have led nowhere. Until he and the people who would be responsible for rolling out the sponsorship could actually see what a successful Sanex tennis event looked like, it was difficult to advance the conversation. When Frank arrived on site for the Sanex Trophy and saw his brands everywhere, the penny dropped. Discussions on the WTA sponsorship followed soon after.

Frank's small investment endorsing Justine Henin, who was to became a world number one, grew into a sponsorship of the WTA Tour worth $80m – at the time the biggest sponsorship agreement in the history of women's sports. At times it was an agonisingly slow process, but ultimately, by not rushing and by investing time in the relationship, we gained the client's trust, and helped Sara Lee put Sanex on the map in a deal far larger than could have been contemplated at the outset.

Leslie McCormack Gathy

6

Thinking outside the box

... use [street smarts] to get where you want to go,
preferably by the shortest route, even if this means
jumping some fences or going through a few back alleys.

Negotiation is an art rather than a science, and this chapter
shows how thinking creatively and outside the box can create
yet another MHM 'edge'.

Persistence and creativity worked hand in hand when MHM
approached Sony's Masaaki Morita about collaboration. Several
ideas went wide of the mark until one smart new idea hit home,
and the Sony World Golf Rankings were born, the start of a
long professional relationship. For Mr Morita, this relationship
was founded on an 'understanding of our position and [Mark's]
ability to create new concepts'. Being able to **use what you know
about a potential customer or client to create an unusual, new
or unique proposition** is a skill that will reap rewards.

A creative approach helped Wimbledon to come to terms
with MHM's proposal for merchandising and licensing. Trialling
merchandise in Japan – far away from the traditional home of
British tennis – demonstrated the financial and other spin-off
rewards on offer, and paved the way for some completely new
thinking around the Wimbledon brand.

Flexibility can also be a smart negotiating strategy. Sean
McManus recalls a classic MHM masterclass on when and how to
pivot in a situation, occasioned when IMG were faced with a new

competitor on their turf. Partnership rather than confrontation proved to be a solution – but on a basis that reflected IMG's more entrenched position in the market. Even seemingly straightforward negotiations can be transformed when viewed creatively.

Creativity also comes into play when a negotiation is proving to be tricky or has reached an impasse. **Taking a fresh or different approach often works wonders.** The WTA had, for many years, been meeting with the Wimbledon committee to lobby for equal prize money for women when then CEO Larry Scott made a judgement call that inviting Venus Williams to speak on their behalf might help the cause. It did; hearing women tennis players' frustration from a multiple Grand Slam-winning champion turned the tide. If you've taken the time to know and understand with whom you're negotiating and the time seems right, **use ambassadors to support your case.** Bear in mind that people like to do business with people at the top of their game.

Dick Alford similarly reminds us that **an impartial solution can break an impasse**, while Jayne Eiben's youthful naiveté became an asset for IMG when MHM needed to reinforce the value of televising Wimbledon in Hong Kong. Donald Dell praises **the power of pragmatism and common sense**. The point of any negotiation is to reach a mutually advantageous agreement. Don't take refuge in technicalities or legalities and avoid unnecessary showdowns and inflammatory language. They are almost always counter-productive.

Necessity can also be the mother of invention. Financial pressures led to a rethink around accommodating the large IMG team who need to be at Wimbledon each year. The solution of renting an 'IMG house' (now houses) quickly became more than just a cost-saving exercise. And a focus on cost control, as IMG's Caroline Ward tells us, encouraged the company to start bartering with their suppliers, offering brand exposure or sponsorship in return for the services they needed.

That's the kind of outside-the-box thinking that helps you to get ahead in business.

Find a unique proposition

The first time I met Mark I was an executive at Sony. He came to my office in Tokyo with some suggestions as to how we might do business.

His first thought was that we might sponsor a golf tournament in Japan. I said no immediately as other Japanese companies were already involved in sponsoring golf. I explained to him that Sony would only be interested in something that was a unique proposition.

He then suggested sponsorship of the video rights to the Nobel Prize ceremony and speeches given by the recipients of the award. Again, I refused.

His final suggestion was the video rights to the papal world tour. I said that most Japanese people are Buddhist.

I thought then that my first meeting with him would quite possibly be the last. However, a few months later he came back to Japan and invited me to dinner. I agreed as long as we did not discuss any business proposals. We both thoroughly enjoyed the evening and it became a regular event.

After several years of dinners out and tennis games together, Mark mentioned that there was no worldwide golf ranking system and would Sony consider helping him establish one? I said that that was most definitely a unique idea and Sony would probably consider it if the ranking would bear Sony's name. So began the Sony World Golf Rankings. This was followed by the Sony Life Cup Tennis Match.

When I was chairman, president and CEO of Sony Life Insurance company, Mark suggested a Japan vs US women's tennis match, correctly spotting that the women's game in Japan was becoming ever stronger and that interest was growing. I agreed, as, again, an all-female tennis tournament in Japan would be unique. The Sony Life Cup Tennis Match between Japan and the US was held three times in three years in Japan, and was a huge success each time.

Mark would invite me and my wife to the French Open, Wimbledon and the US Open every year. While I watched matches on Centre Court, I wondered why there were never any Japanese players there. So in 2000, after retiring from Sony group, I established the Masaaki Morita Tennis Fund. My aim was to support Japanese junior tennis players, in the hope that one day, I would see one of them playing on Centre Court at Wimbledon.

I wanted to select young Japanese junior players who displayed unique character and potential, and send them to the best training camp abroad. However, I had no knowledge of tennis training camps. I called Mark and explained my idea, asking for his recommendation. Mark said that IMG had recently taken over the best tennis camp in the world, the Nick Bollettieri Tennis Academy (now the IMG Academy). He shared my idea with Nick and asked for his support. Nick promised to help and the Fund was established. Kei Nishikori benefitted from the Fund and rose to become the world number four player and a US Open finalist in 2014. And he also played on Wimbledon's Centre Court.

Without Mark's recommendation and support, I would not have been able to train Kei at the IMG Academy, which was really the key to the success of the project.

Under the leadership of its founder, Mr Ibuka, Sony Corporation's philosophy was to be truly innovative, and to do things that no one had ever done before. Rather than copying other products, we were challenged to innovate and as a result we developed new products such as the world's first transistor radio, compact disc and Walkman.

Every one of my business dealings with Mark was centred around a unique proposition. His entrepreneurial and innovative approach chimed with our philosophy at Sony. Through his understanding of our position and his ability to create new concepts, he was able to marry our two worlds together and as a result, everything that we did together was a success.

Masaaki Morita

Think creatively

Creativity is not one of my strengths, which is why I admire it so much in other people. Mark introducing Wimbledon to the concept of licensing and merchandising was one such example. Back in the late seventies, it was not something the AELTC had thought of at all. We were entirely focused on running Wimbledon and promoting a tennis tournament, and that was our core business. While we understood television and presence agreements, we didn't see ourselves as a brand that could be exploited. Mark introduced a fundamental change to our way of thinking.

We were nervous and cautious about it at first, as it didn't seem logical to us. No other sports agent was involved with merchandising at this stage. We tried to weigh up the pluses and minuses and in the end there didn't seem many minuses. Mark suggested that we start in Japan, as he knew the Japanese market well and also knew that its geographical distance from Wimbledon would make us more comfortable. If it didn't work, no one need know about it.

In fact, it was successful from the outset. We started with the more familiar territory of tennis apparel and shoes, but Mark suggested that we extend the merchandising programme to special items like jewellery and leather goods. He introduced the Flying W logo, which could be put on smaller items to extend our range.

For a long period, we were very successful in Japan. By 2005 we had around 24 shops in eight international markets. The revenue was a bonus, but the rewards went beyond the financial: it brought Wimbledon to the attention of the Far East. Raising Wimbledon's profile helped with our television agreements. Renown, our main clothing company in Japan, took advertising slots in Japanese television programmes promoting Wimbledon and that all added to our success.

It was undoubtedly a good decision, implemented brilliantly

by Mark. He was so ahead of the game. His creative thinking changed how Wimbledon perceives its brand. Merchandising and licensing continue to support and enhance how Wimbledon delivers its core activities.

Chris Gorringe

Know when (and how) to pivot

Knowing when to be flexible while negotiating is a skill that can reap dividends. Mark had the talent to pivot on a deal when necessary. Back in the 1990s, there was an ABC Sports golf producer who was attempting to get into the golf event management business, clearly something that Mark thought should be the private domain of IMG.

The producer was trying to create a network golf event for the same weekend that we were. He had ABC lined up and we had NBC. We were fighting over sponsors, site fees, golfers, television time, and Mark put me in charge of working with our golf division to, quite frankly, squash the other event. No one was more competitive in these situations than Mark. It soon became apparent that, due in part to IMG's access to top players and NBC's strong backing, the IMG event would be a better event. However, the other event would still take place, weakening ours considerably.

I had an early morning meeting to update Mark on my progress and where things stood, but before I could even finish my synopsis, he interrupted with, 'why don't we partner with this man on this event?', realising that bringing a potential competitor into the tent was probably better than having him as a thorn in our side for years to come. So I figured I would pivot along with Mark and said, optimistically: 'Maybe you're right, owning 50 per cent of a great event is probably better than 100 per cent of a mediocre one.' He frowned and replied, 'Who said anything about 50/50? Start at 75/25 and accept 70/30.' A partnership was a sensible option, but there was no point in ceding more of IMG's territory than was necessary. Knowing when to pivot is an important part of negotiation; knowing how is an even greater skill.

Sean McManus

Choose the right advocates

For 37 years, every CEO of the WTA (Women's Tennis Association) had gone into a meeting with the Wimbledon committee to advocate for equal prize money. When I was president and Larry Scott was chairman and CEO, Venus Williams had started talking to us, saying that she wanted to get more involved and to help contribute more off court. She was on the player council and had already provided great leadership for the players and the sport overall. Larry took a chance. He said that she should come along to the next Wimbledon committee meeting, which was on the eve of her Grand Slam final. He said that no one was more articulate or passionate about equal prize money, and to hear the words from a Wimbledon champion would be powerful. Venus went into the boardroom, which was all male bar one, and told them to hold hands and close their eyes. She asked them to imagine being a little girl, growing up and practising as hard as she can. She fights and works, and makes sacrifices. And then she gets to this stage and is told she's not the same as a boy. Almost as good, but not quite. How devastating and demoralising would that be?

Venus's strategy and management of that moment was very symbolic and effective. The public opinion polls in France and the UK supported us, the UK prime minister and sports minister supported us, and London was bidding for the 2012 Olympic Games at the time, so there was a constellation, a moment of real opportunity. Larry had seen the potential impact that Venus's appearance could have. She helped us achieve what so many

WTA athletes and administrators had championed for decades. The last mile is the toughest and she was there leading the charge for everyone in women's tennis. We could not have had a better champion advocating for change.

Stacey Allaster

Play your joker

Sometimes it takes something out of the ordinary to break an impasse or to change the pace in a negotiation. Rolex were already on board with Wimbledon and the time for their contract renewal was coming up. Seiko had been approached and had come up with an offer that was considerably more than Rolex's, who refused to budge from the figure they had put forward. Mark knew that Rolex was a fantastic fit for Wimbledon in terms of brand, but he also had an obligation to maximise profits for the AELTC. It was a difficult situation and the question was how to get over the impasse.

Mark invited André Heiniger, chairman of Rolex, over for dinner with the Wimbledon committee, knowing what a charming and gregarious man he was and what fantastic presence he had. During the dinner, André gave a ten-minute speech explaining why Wimbledon and Rolex should be together as they complemented each other entirely. He talked of their shared values, expertise, quality and longevity. He didn't refer to Seiko or anyone else. He had no need to. He had addressed all the points that were important to Wimbledon and that would give them peace of mind. Following on from that dinner, the deal went through with Rolex, despite the lesser sum offered. The smart play had been to understand how the committee would react to André, and to bring him into the negotiation at the right time.

Ian Todd

An impartial voice

When discussions are going nowhere, and neither side seems prepared to budge, look for the impartial solution that will appease both sides.

I had been back at IMG for just over a year, having spent some time working for McCann Erickson. Out of the blue I got a phone call from Peter Smith, a senior IMG executive, who had just come from a big IMG dinner in Hong Kong. Peter told me that the focal point of discussions that evening had been the company's interest in moving into India. There was clearly a lot of potential, with a country obsessed by its national sport, cricket. But, Peter explained, there had been huge disagreement about how this move should be managed and who should be in charge. There was a battle between the London office, who saw it as their area of expertise given their ties with India and their knowledge of cricket, and the Hong Kong office, who felt that, geographically, it made sense that it came under their control.

Throughout the course of the dinner, both sides had put forward their arguments, with neither side prepared to budge. The impasse was threatening to jeopardise the whole venture. As the arguments were batted forwards and back, Mark sat there, listening, without saying a word. Having listened intently for some time, he then interjected, saying that he had a suggestion. What is required, he continued, is someone new, who is not working in either Hong Kong or London, but who knows the whole IMG system, someone who may not necessarily be a cricket expert but who knows a lot about tennis and golf and who would be able to build up a client base in those areas. And then he suggested me. This was a typical Mark intervention, outside-the-box thinking that resolved a seemingly intractable situation while keeping everyone on board. An impartial solution is often very powerful.

Dick Alford

Youthful naiveté can help in tough negotiations

In the spring of 1988 and unbeknown to me, IMG's negotiations in Hong Kong for the television rights to Wimbledon had acrimoniously stalled. The local English-speaking television station refused to pay more and IMG refused to accept less than a hefty increase in the yearly licensing fee.

Coinciding with this impasse, my phone rang at IMG headquarters in Cleveland, where I worked as a young account executive. It was Mark calling to ask what I was working on. I explained that I had mentioned to my boss that I was looking for a new assignment. Just before the end of the day, he called again with a directive. I was to fly to London immediately for a briefing on an assignment in Hong Kong. When I mentioned that I had not been there before, he laughed and said enigmatically, 'Great … that qualifies you for what I want you to do.'

In London I learned that negotiations over the television rights in Hong Kong had collapsed. Consequently, Mark had decided to end the yearly broadcast of Wimbledon in Hong Kong and instead screen it on closed-circuit television at an exclusive location. My job was to organise and plan an event at a hotel where expatriate Brits could – for a hefty price – comfortably watch the tournament.

At the time, I had no idea that taking Wimbledon off television in Hong Kong would be akin to taking the Super Bowl off the air in America and converting it to pay-per-view at the Ritz. As public discontent grew, a local radio station invited me on air to talk about Wimbledon. Hoping to pitch the event more positively, I readily agreed. It proved to be a disaster, with angry listeners calling in to berate me. All my arguments proved unpersuasive and what was worse, I had still only sold three tickets.

The day after this humiliation, Mark called me and he seemed cheerful, telling me that he had thoroughly enjoyed the interview. I could not work out how he knew about it (these were pre-internet days) or why he was laughing. I felt he must be omniscient. I didn't bother to mention that I'd sold only three tickets as I figured he knew that too.

Within weeks the public uproar in Hong Kong had reached fever pitch. Feeling the heat, the local television station capitulated and agreed to pay the higher price for the rights to air Wimbledon, which meant that I could return home. Mark had won another game of business hardball. The agreed-upon licensing fee that year was in the mid-five figures and within just a few years had risen to the mid-six figures.

I think there were a number of reasons why I was sent to organise this doomed event. Mark didn't want to damage the careers and reputations of any of IMG's Hong Kong employees. I was the sacrificial lamb, loathed by locals but able to leave unscathed. Secondly, he believed my naiveté and youthful determination would convince the television station that IMG would never back down.

Finally, he enjoyed dispensing life lessons and unforgettable experiences to young, eager minions. Now, whenever someone at work says that our goals are too high or a project is too difficult or stressful, I remember my days with IMG and Mark and laugh. 'Trust me,' I always say, 'We can do this!'

Jayne Eiben

Taking a creative spin

In the winter of 1979–80 the European Tour succeeded in having BBC television sign a multi-year rights deal for numerous tournaments. We had struck an agreement with the new head of sport at the BBC, for whom restoring coverage of the Ryder Cup was a key objective. We were able to use this as a lever to try to get a commitment from the BBC to cover as many golf tournaments as possible. The more network coverage we could guarantee, the greater the prospect of getting big sponsors and hence more prize money. In the end, we secured a four-year contract that included the Ryder Cup and a raft of other tournaments. That left the World Match Play as the odd one out. After the Open, the World Match Play was the biggest event in European golf, but the Tour had no part of it financially. Historically, IMG held all the rights.

When I met up with Mark he congratulated me on having negotiated the BBC arrangement. I thanked him before quickly following up with, 'Mark, we now need to talk about the Tour receiving its share of the World Match Play TV rights. We have all the other events properly under the Tour's control. We need to be brought into this contract.' I suggested, firmly but fairly, that 50 per cent would be appropriate. Mark said he would think about it and get back to me.

A little while later, Mark called and said, 'Ken, you made a fair point, and I think 50 per cent is about right.' I felt quite elated having got Mark, the ultimate negotiator, to agree to my terms. Then he continued: 'We can offer 10 per cent now, 20 per cent in year two, 30 per cent in year three, 40 per cent in year four, and then 50 per cent in year five.'

I had no comeback – Mark would let us have our 50 per cent but not for five more years. In fact it was a beautiful solution. It answered in the positive that the Tour was right and should participate in and benefit from the World Match Play Championship. And it enabled us to look other promoters and sponsors in the eye and say that we had now regularised all of the events. It was another lesson for me in the art of creative negotiation.

Ken Schofield

Common sense often makes the most sense

After I sold ProServ to SFX Sports Group, I continued working for SFX in their sports division. One day, Mark called and asked me to meet him. It transpired that SFX had bought a company from Dick Button, the ice-skating champion. The company had created a sports show that ran on US television. When SFX bought the company, they also bought that show. However, the programme had been created with Barry Frank, IMG's senior TV guy, who had been responsible for running it and securing sponsorship. The SFX people had been talking to the IMG people and trying to figure out who owned what and who would be running what, and the negotiations were getting nowhere.

It was clearly frustrating Mark, and that was the reason he had asked to see me. When we met, he had a proposition for me: that I should talk to my SFX colleagues and ask them to make IMG a fair proposal to resolve the impasse. He said that he would accept whatever I came back with. I was slightly shocked, because I knew that I was conflicted, but despite that conflict he trusted me to be fair and to try to help him work with SFX. Otherwise, he would just pull back, change the name of the show, bring the sponsor along, organise the event and sell it to the network without any SFX involvement.

I knew that Mark was correct, and that his suggestion made a lot of sense. I said OK and went back to the SFX people involved. However, as much as I tried to get them to come up with a fair and reasonable offer rather than risk losing the show, they refused and wanted to get back to the negotiating table with IMG, to thrash out the details. We went round and round in circles but eventually I had to go back to Mark and say that I couldn't do it. And sure enough, we lost the show. IMG and the sponsor decided to go it alone, and set up a new programme, with a new title. Talking common sense rather than legalities, and taking a pragmatic view is often the way out of a tricky situation.

Donald Dell

Find a unique solution

With tennis an important cornerstone of IMG's business, the Wimbledon fortnight became an important fixture, with lots of out-of-town executives descending on London for two weeks of meetings and to support their clients. With an astute focus on cutting costs whenever possible, my dad quickly realised that the expense involved in housing executives in central London hotels could be colossal. The solution was at the time unique: rent a house in Wimbledon from one of the many residents looking to avoid the chaos that descends on the village during The Championships.

For IMG, we not only saved money, we gained on convenience, quality of accommodation and even team building. Executives staying on site could walk to the courts and into Wimbledon village. A cook was brought in to cater breakfast, lunch and dinner. The public areas of the house were also used for entertaining, providing a welcome refuge from the tournament or a place to wait out a lengthy rain delay.

IMG now rents several houses during the Wimbledon fortnight and most of its competitors do the same. Imitation is the greatest form of flattery, and in this case proof positive that thinking creatively about a problem, especially one that might be expensive, can provide a solution that is both cheaper and more appealing for everyone involved.

Leslie McCormack Gathy

SHORT SMART

Mark said that he would always have his driver pick him up from the departures area of an airport rather than the arrivals, as the departures is always much less crowded. He was absolutely right and it is something I do regularly.

Peter McKelvey

The power of barter

Barter deals made a huge difference to IMG's finances. With so many people buzzing around the world, the company needed to be an intelligent buyer of services and funnel its expenditure down the same channels in order to make the most of any deals that had been done. In our case, we made a very effective use of barter deals. Mark set up the Administrative Operations Committee (AOC) to look at those items on which we were spending the most across all departments. Divisional managers were asked from whom they bought those products and services, and were then charged with doing either a barter deal or some form of sponsorship deal.

There were many companies that wanted marketing exposure in connection with our clients who might not have had the marketing budget but who could contribute by offering services. BMW would perhaps offer a fleet of courtesy cars for an event in return for a couple of pages in the programme, with a mention as an approved supplier. Similarly with our photocopier supplier. One of our biggest deals was with Lufthansa. In return for exposure at events, we had thousands of dollars worth of flights we could use. We saved ourselves a whole lot of expenditure each year by taking a more creative approach to buying in services.

Caroline Ward

SHORT SMART

Only read a memo, email or document once. On one occasion I saw Mark board a plane with a stack of memos. Once each one was read, he would either make notes on it and put it on the right, or rip it up and put it on the left. He came off the plane with four or five pieces of paper having gone on with 50. We have a tendency to half-read something then put it aside, or read it but not really concentrate. Now when I read a memo, I really concentrate while I am reading it and I don't have to go back to it a number of times.

Timo Lumme

PART 3

Growing a business

7

Setting culture and values

A lot of building a business is listening to your own common sense, then taking the necessary steps to turn the theories into practice.

As with so many other things, MHM took a common-sense approach to growing a business. He noted in a typically no-nonsense way in *What They Don't Teach You …* that IMG's success was down to nothing that was 'all that unique or unconventional'. Such modesty belies his wisdom around building and maintaining a business that has motivated generations of business leaders since. It's clear that this thinking and practice also influenced our contributors, whether at IMG or beyond. Part 3 of *Beyond Harvard* tells the stories of how MHM helped them to create their own business success.

Chapter 7 focuses on the values and ethos you should bring to growing a business. IMG's Sam Zussman firmly believes that 'you cannot be a market leader in any industry without values'. For him, the Harvards and Stanfords of this world focus on the mechanics – the *tangibles* – of business, while MHM's approach was based on the *intangibles*, the principles and values that he was able both to describe and prescribe so eloquently. **Values and principles are an important business underpinning.** Motown's Berry Gordy never worked in the same industry as MHM, but their friendship was founded on a shared principles-based approach to business, a desire for the people they were promoting 'to have character and honour, humility and passion, and to thrive on competition'.

The values you bring to business will also determine the *type* of business you want to grow, as Sir Martin Sorrell explains. But once you've decided on an approach, it's important to keep your focus. **Be professional at all times, and set the highest possible standards** for yourself and the people you work with. Commit to quality. Don't overlook the details. Play to win, but do so with your integrity intact. Gavin Forbes reminds us that **reputation is everything in business**, both for organisations and the individuals who represent them.

Ingraining your corporate culture with common values will ensure that you present a powerful image in the markets in which you operate. **Lead and teach by example**. For Bob Kain, being able to watch and learn from people at the top of their game was 'mentoring by example', an approach that permeated the whole of the company. Catherine Simpson shows us how this kind of inclusive, 'can-do' culture has helped IMG to expand and thrive internationally.

Principles, values and culture also find expression in business vision and structures. Think carefully about the structures that will work for your business – do you need stricter compartmentalisation or fluidity and flexibility? – but **never let structure become a straitjacket or restrict innovation or growth**. MHM's famous multi-division approach at IMG enabled him to see across a fairly flat business organisation and, crucially, to make connections across the landscape. Jeremy Palmer-Tomkinson believes that IMG's open and accessible structure and culture was crucial to its ability to diversify.

Jeni Rose has worked in the modelling industry for her whole career and was struck when IMG entered the market by their innate sense of doing business professionally and ethically, something she believes has both supported the success of IMG Models and influenced the industry as a whole. For her, an ethical approach is 'a driver for us all'. **Acting with integrity**

and focusing on the 'greater good' is good for business and often for the people it touches. Sebastian Coe reminds us that fears about the commercialisation of sport must be balanced by the greater good that financial support can provide for athletes and their families.

Espousing an inclusive, principles-based approach does not, of course, create a culture immune to business discipline. Keep an eye on the detail and find ways to reinforce important messages around running a tight ship. Gavin Forbes will never forget being reminded by MHM himself about tipping; Jeni Rose thinks fondly of MHM every time she follows his advice on saving incoming paper clips. Howard Katz reminds us that while emotion can generate creativity and enthusiasm for new business, you also need to be hard-headed when things don't go as planned: 'Sometimes in business you need to know when to pull the plug, no matter how much you've invested – both emotionally and financially … Failure is unfortunately just part of business. The trick is to **learn from that failure and move on as cleanly as possible.**'

Wise words. Read on for more.

Make the most of your core values

You cannot be a market leader in any industry without values. If you don't care about your reputation or your customers, if you take a short-sighted view, if you don't invest in relationships or build trust and respect, you don't last. I'm sure that some organisations could muscle their way through by aggression, capital and market position for a certain period of time, but, longer term, these things come back to haunt you.

Mark didn't make these core values up. They are empirical truths. When Newton witnessed gravity, he didn't invent it, it was already there. But he was the first one who noticed it and verbalised it and defined it. Similarly, Mark was able to figure out the importance of these values, what the elements were and how to verbalise them. He was perceptive and self-observant. For him, the education system – the Harvards or Stanfords of this world – focused on the mechanics, the tangibles of business, while his approach came from experience, and a focus on the intangibles. He would verbalise his perceptions in a way that would make the intangible more tangible. In that way, he could help others to grasp these elements, appreciate them and attempt to be better at them.

If you asked an athlete about how they threw a ball, they would say, 'I don't know, I picked it up and threw it.' They might be great but not understand why. If you took that same person and gave them the ability to learn more about the way that they throw, they would do even better. Great executives have a tangible and intangible side and these have to complement each other. Some things come easier to us than others, and while there are textbooks to learn the tangible side, it is harder to grasp the intangible. We all aspire to be better versions of ourselves, and Mark did a great service by providing a helping hand.

I never met Mark, but I believe that these principles and values came naturally to him, and that he lived and breathed them. His skill was in both describing and prescribing them. He described clearly what he believed should be empirically true, and he prescribed in the sense that everything he did and everyone he brought into IMG was prescribed in that image.

When you come across IMG alumni, you have this ease of comfort and confidence that they 'get it'. I have often rehired people who were here in a more junior capacity because I know that they understand these core values, the intangibles they possess, because they were here before. There is something in the DNA of the company that Mark imprinted years before and is still absolutely core to the company today.

Sam Zussman

Principles matter

What could a white Yale law graduate from Chicago and a black high-school dropout from Detroit possibly have in common in the philosophy of business? I found that out many years ago when I met Mark McCormack at a tennis match. I found him fascinating. He liked me too. We became fast friends.

Even though we worked in different industries, and managed different types of people, we shared the same philosophy – principles matter. We wanted the people we were promoting to have character and honour, humility and passion, and to thrive on competition.

The more Mark and I talked, the more we realised that we were both trying to do the same thing – make our people superstars. We shared thoughts, ideas and philosophies. I had heard that, when Mark first met a client, if he didn't think they had the character and dedication to go all the way, he would not sign them. After all, his academy nurtured his clients for many years.

At Motown, I led the same way. Michael Jackson and Stevie Wonder were no more than eight or ten, and Diana Ross and the Supremes and Smokey Robinson were about seventeen when we met. But in addition to their talent, I had to see the right character to sign them.

I had great respect for Mark's approach and would ask him, 'How do you do it with so many different types of people?' They were all over the place – golf, football, basketball, fashion, you name it. He would say, 'If people, no matter what field they're in, have the right principles, they give themselves a much better chance of winning in this world. Our job is to make them aware of that.'

I came up as a black man in a world where white disc jockeys would not play my music. My idea for Motown was making music for *all* people. I had to convince them that all people had the same emotions – wanted the same things in life, had the same concerns and fears.

Mark had the same feelings and dealt with people the same way I did – trying to make his clients the best they could be regardless of the colour of their skin or where they came from.

Looking back, we knew we were extremely lucky. We felt grateful because we shared a strong love for the people and the businesses we worked in. I started as a songwriter who didn't have the voice to be a singer but loved to teach, develop and promote those who did. Mark was a great college golfer who missed the cut for the 1958 US Open, but turned his love of sports into a management career signing golfers like Arnold Palmer, Jack Nicklaus, Gary Player and Tiger Woods, tennis greats like Chris Evert and Bjorn Borg, and so many others.

I loved to hear Mark's take on his philosophies for promoting an artist, while keeping them from going down the wrong track. He agreed with me that direction is much more important than speed. If you are going fast and fly off track, into the weeds or jungle, it takes a long time to get back. If you stay on the straight and narrow, you get there much faster.

Mark McCormack was a pioneer who left a monumental footprint in the world of sports, management and media. He was a brilliant businessman and, most definitely, as he demonstrated through his consistent business philosophy … *a man of principle*.

Berry Gordy

Grow the business you want

Once a business has moved beyond its start-up phase, the owner needs to make decisions as to the type of business it will become – important choices over issues such as size and control will need to be made, and these need to be led by character.

Some people are good at starting companies and then sell them in order that they can try something else. Others are good at growing companies, and, when they try to start their own without the resources and infrastructure of a larger company, it proves a disaster. It is unusual for people to do both. The qualities that are needed to start something are very different from those needed to build something of scale.

Mark believed in rigid technical control, and if you stick to those beliefs and run a company along those lines, there are consequences. His philosophy meant that there were limits to its scale. Mark could have grown IMG into a much greater entity but he was happy to sacrifice size for personal control. He lived and breathed the business. Everything he did was for the business, and it was an extension of his personality. I don't think he would have been comfortable in a public company environment and the exposure to the searchlight and loss of control that that would have entailed. The irony is that these days, Mark Zuckerberg controls Facebook, Larry Page and Sergey Brin control Google, and Jeff Bezos controls Amazon, as institutional investors now accept that structures can be put in place in public companies allowing individuals to retain control.

Mark would have been even more phenomenal with scale. While the business was big within its industry, its image was bigger than the reality. Mark was good at creating that impression. He never talked about profitability or revenues but always the number of people employed and the number of offices around the world. We have the reverse set-up. Nobody knows that WPP is the 25th largest company in the UK or 271st in the world.

It comes down to different approaches and different ideals. I always found *What They Don't Teach You at Harvard Business School* heretical. I think my time spent at Harvard framed my attitude and made it at odds with his. My mother said that my attending Harvard was the worst thing that ever happened to me because it made me too business-focused. I sat there listening to three case studies every day and trying to analyse what the chairman/CEO should do and why, and it made me think very strategically and become a believer in scale.

Mark, however, I am sure thought that owning 100 per cent

of IMG was better than owning 2 per cent of WPP, which is about how our holdings compared. To Mark, control was very important, and he may be right, as then you control your destiny. In my opinion, the pity of it is that if he had had a different approach, he could have been even more spectacular. But there is no right or wrong. The important thing is to recognise what is important to you as you grow your business.

Sir Martin Sorrell

Keep your focus

Focus is a key element of success. It struck me every time I was with Mark. His attention to detail and focus was phenomenal. He had his 3 × 5 cards in his pocket and was always taking notes. He never missed a trick, no matter what we were talking about. If he liked a joke you told him he would write down the punchline to jog his memory. If I mentioned a name that I thought might be useful, a sports star for example, it was written down and he was on the case the next day. If I mentioned anything I was thinking of doing, he would put that idea together with an opportunity and follow up religiously. There would be a letter in the post straightaway.

When I launched Fiji Water, for example, he connected me with the golfer Vijay Singh, who is a Fijian, and I went down to Miami to meet him at a tournament. He also connected me with Gary Player, who is a great communicator and passionate about health. Gary used to drink water between holes, and if he saw any child spectating who was drinking a Coke, he would go over and give them a bottle of Fiji Water instead.

Mark wouldn't think in terms of wanting to be in any other business. He focused on one area and that focus created an empire. Anything he did he would have been successful at, but at IMG he was über-successful because he lived and breathed the business. He was brilliant because he focused so much on this one area and built it up. He expanded and expanded that one gem of an idea that he had hatched with Arnold Palmer. He applied his expertise to non-sports personalities with similar needs in the worlds of modelling and classical music but he would not have been as successful if he had diversified outside his realm of expertise. It was extraordinary that he was never persuaded to start something else, like the manufacture of tennis rackets.

The lesson to draw is: don't overstretch yourself. Mark was brilliant because he kept focused on his area of expertise. Diversification would have been a mistake. Chris Evert once explained to Mark the importance of focus, saying that in the Ladies Final at Wimbledon, she watched the ball hit her racket face; she didn't watch the scoreboard. And that's how she won. There was no fear or distraction, just focus. Mark brought this same approach to IMG and his approach paid dividends.

David Gilmour

Look to the details for long-term growth

The key quality that permeated everything Mark said and did was his complete dedication to detail and focus. I have immense respect for people with those traits because they are the people who get things done.

It is evident in the way he created and built IMG. Here was a man who bumped against Arnold Palmer and over a handshake decided to start a business. He then painstakingly put the group together, division by division, quality people by quality people, overseeing every step. Steadily, and with an absolute focus on what he was doing, he created something that wasn't just a moment in time. It didn't just create a big magnesium flash and then fizzle out. It continued to grow and grow, and, with each year, to change the landscape even further. Through focus and attention to detail, he built a business that didn't just dominate, but became the blueprint for everything else we have done in the sports business.

I understand that mentality better than most because I am similar. I'm only ever thinking about the next challenge – if we do this, what will be the implications? Everything I have successfully achieved has been because of my obsession with detail. You can't deliver the Olympic Games for seven years without sitting there trying to figure out, on an hour-by-hour basis, how to do something better and to make sure that what you are asking to be done is actually being executed. It is the same in a sporting career. You can leave absolutely no stone unturned. You don't want to be confronted in an Olympic final with anything you haven't confronted on a training track a thousand times before. For me, it's the same mentality, an obsession with detail, which contributes to enduring success.

Sebastian Coe

Sweat the small stuff

When I was studying for an MBA at Harvard, Mark and his development of IMG was one of the case studies, under the heading Management of New Enterprises. Mark came in to give a talk, and in it he said that he had learned an important lesson from Lew Wasserman, a US talent agent who eventually went on to run the Music Corporation of America (MCA). Lew acted for, among others, a famous composer and conductor and he maintained that, even at the height of his powers, he was never too proud to order a baton for that composer.

Mark said that, for him, it was not just a question of negotiating some big contract for Arnold Palmer. If Arnold said he needed a pair of size eight golf shoes for the tournament tomorrow, Mark would get them. It was hugely instructive. It taught me to not just look at the big picture but also the smallest details. The devil is in the detail. Some people will call that micro-management in a slightly derogatory fashion, but I take it as a compliment. If you extract yourself from the detail, it is very difficult to get back into it. Extracting yourself from the operation in that way is something neither Mark nor I would do; the detail matters much too much.

Sir Martin Sorrell

Pursue perfection

As a brand, Rolex is known for its measured and precise approach, always striving for perfection. Mark was very similar, which was why we were a good fit for each other. He was passionate about sport, and I believe was led by his heart, but he always had a structured, precise, rational approach, and he aimed for perfection. These traits were in evidence in his personal life as well as his business one, as they were completely interlinked.

I would meet Mark in London, New York, Paris or Geneva and he clearly spent a lot of time staying in hotels. He once told me that to save time in the morning he knew exactly where he put his stuff to brush his hair and his teeth, or to clean his face. He would stay in the same hotel in the same room so he knew the layout exactly. It was all part of a specific routine that had to be adhered to. 'But now,' he complained, 'a new maid moves things around every morning. If she moves my stuff from here to there I am lost! I have been to see the manager and if she keeps doing it I'm going to have to move hotels.' He had the same approach to his leisure time. Mark had been a very good golfer but over time played less and less and started to play tennis instead. I asked him why he had stopped playing when he was so good.

'I played a couple of months ago on a course that I know very well,' he replied. 'I knew I needed to hit a shot on the fairway that would go low and right. I played the shot and instead it went high and left. I thought: I know exactly how to play that shot and yet I didn't manage it. If there is such a disconnect between my body and my mind, I'm not prepared to go on.'

It was possibly his only poor shot of the day, but he was shocked that he had not been able to deliver to his own exacting standards. These standards were an integral part of Mark's success, including the strong relationship with Rolex over many years. Although Mark's standards may seem unreasonably high to many, pursuing perfection should always be a goal.

Bertrand Gros

Be professional at all times

I signed with IMG when I was eighteen. I was drawn to the company because they were the biggest in the world, they were professional and they had a good reputation. They also had a global presence, which appealed to me because I was interested in being a global player. It meant that if I travelled to the US, Australia or Japan or anywhere in the world, I would have someone to take care of me as soon as I arrived. When playing in Japan, for example, I needed a translator, and that was all dealt with.

The professional approach that ran through IMG stemmed from Mark. We were once in Berlin designing the Berlin Sporting Club, a three 18-hole complex with each course designed by myself, Arnold Palmer and Nick Faldo respectively. We were talking to a company about some aspect of the design or construction, and although the discussions came to nothing, they ended amicably. Mark said to me that his philosophy was always to treat people in a way that you can come back to them at some later date. Things can change in a heartbeat, so never burn your bridges by leaving a bad impression, and possibly losing the opportunity of ever working with that company again. To me it was common sense, but that is often the best advice, and it was good to hear it from Mark.

After I won my first major when I was 27, I was advised by my agent at IMG that, from that point on, I just had to live a clean life. Don't do anything stupid that might damage your image, say the right things, smile, continue to play decent golf and you will do well, he said. Coupled with that, he advised that I should aim to be an ambassador for four or five blue-chip companies rather than setting up 25 deals with lesser companies just to earn a quick buck; the wisdom of that approach has always stuck with me. I would rather just be associated with the best car, the best watch or the best clothing company. If you represent a number of products, the audience gets confused and the message that you are trying to convey becomes diluted. The two pieces of advice go hand in hand, as the best or most prestigious companies only want to associate with the best sportspeople – both on and off the course. People take note of a professional approach long after the last putt or the end of a business meeting.

Bernhard Langer

Set the standard

In a client-facing business, it is crucial that you are seen to be going the extra mile, and not at risk of becoming complacent. That is the culture at IMG that stemmed from Mark's approach. Many of IMG's clients are long-standing because IMG continues to deliver. It would be easy to run a successful golf tournament and then sit back on our laurels and think 'that worked well, let's do that again'. But instead you must continually innovate, constantly look at your performance and see how it could be improved, because if you are not moving forwards, you are moving backwards.

One of the most important elements of service delivery is that sponsors are kept happy. I ran a tournament during which we were going to offer a car for any player who got a hole in one. The tournament was played in March, and the previous November we sent out leaflets to try to sell tickets, flagging up the hole-in-one prize. Two months before the competition the car sponsor dropped out and we duly sent out a release to the media saying that the car would no longer be offered. When the tournament finally started, the first day proved to be a damp squib. The stars were not performing, and the weather was bad. The only bit of news that the media could latch on to was that one fairly unknown pro holed in one. They jumped on it, and suddenly the talk was of the pro receiving a car, when we had no car to give. Even though we had alerted the media to the change well in advance, there was a serious risk of negative publicity impacting the event, and tarnishing our main sponsors. Any protracted discussions with the media about who was right or wrong would not have done them any favours. With the president of our sponsor due to fly in the next day, there was nothing for it but for me to rush down to the car dealers, buy a car and present it to the pro.

In the early days of sports marketing, IMG had little competition and represented most of the key players. We could offer to run a tournament anywhere in the world and virtually guarantee that we would bring the best players. But Mark was careful that IMG did not abuse that dominance. Wherever we did run a tournament, we ran it to the best of our ability and went the extra mile to make sure that we delivered. The sports marketing industry these days is much more complicated, with many more agents and sports companies representing the top golfers. However, IMG still has a significant advantage because of its track record in service delivery. I have run some 300 tournaments in 40 different countries. I have trained people who now run tournaments for us, and although these events are much more complicated than before we still practise to the same exacting standards as those stipulated in the early days of IMG.

Peter German

Integrity always outweighs short-term gain

I spend some time teaching sports law at the University of Virgina (UVA) law school. Having taught for fifteen years, and seen how things work, in my first class I now say to the students: 'If you never see me again, if you choose not to take my class and go to another, or if you come to class and don't participate or remember a single case, just remember two words. "Trust" and "Relationships". If you can build on those two concepts you will be a success in law or business.'

Mark and I both believed that, and knew how important each of those concepts is, regardless of who you are dealing with.

I had someone at ProServ who was very close to me, but with whom I had a huge falling-out. He said he was going to leave and set up somewhere else. In reality, that never happens. People do not set up on their own – they always try to take two or three key clients. This person approached IMG offering to bring three top clients with him if he was hired. The first I knew of it was when I was driving on vacation with my wife and two children. My car phone rang and I picked it up. This voice said: 'Donald, it's Mark. Don't say anything. So and so has been up here to see us three times. I know he's very close to you, but don't worry, IMG will never, ever hire him out of respect to you. Thank you. Bye.'

The whole call was less than 30 seconds but it was remarkable. If we had got into a lawsuit he didn't want the phone call to be a matter of public record, so there was no conversation – I just listened. But the most important point was that Mark wouldn't hire this person or take advantage of the situation no matter what. Trust and relationships matter in all areas of business.

Donald Dell

Ingrain your values into corporate culture

As should be the case with pretty much any business, honesty and integrity are fundamental values at IMG. Mark set huge store by the notion that his word was his bond, and wouldn't tolerate any form of dishonesty in the company, no matter how trivial. He had a particular way of making sure that these values were being driven through IMG.

Sitting at my desk one day I had a call from Mark. During the conversation, he said, 'How are we doing with the young girl from Minnesota?' It was an innocuous question, and it would have been easy enough to just say, 'fine', and carry on. But I picked Mark up on what I knew was a mistake and said, 'Mark, she's not from Minnesota, she is from California.' Quick as a flash, he came back with, 'I know, I was just checking.' I had just passed the 'McCormack test'. If he called you or even bumped into you in a lift and asked a question to which you didn't know the answer, it was fine. If you said, 'I'll find out as quickly as I can and get back to you,' that was fine. But if you tried to cover yourself with a lie, you had failed. He would immediately lose respect for you. There weren't many second chances for people who failed the test. I know one guy who was asked a question and took a guess at the answer. He was wrong, and never really progressed beyond the lower levels of the company.

These trick questions were a means of trying to see who was honest and who was not in the way that they operated. Mark's theory was that we are in this business for the long run. If you don't tell people the truth or you do a one-sided deal, word spreads and you lose your reputation in a flash. It was a great lesson. We have had instances where people have not fitted the mould and I would like to think we have weeded that out. I have been in this industry for 30 years, and at the end of the day, I am only as good as my reputation.

Gavin Forbes

Teach by example

Mark taught me so much, not by being a teacher giving formal lessons, but just by being what and who he was and my being able to observe him and watch him in action. It took me years to realise how much I had learned from him. When our bid to host the Olympics in Albertville was successful, I became co-president of the Organising Committee of the 1992 Olympic Winter Games. Suddenly I was a businessman, head of an enterprise with 24,000 people working for me. Mark and IMG did such a good job managing my own career that I hired them to help run the marketing programme for the Albertville Games. I surprised myself every day. I would say to myself, 'How did I know that?', about advertising, or sponsorship, or whatever, and then I realised that most of it was from Mark. And the Games were a huge success.

It wasn't just practical things that I learned but also an approach to life. I have Mark in my head somewhere and I carry so many things that he has given me that, in that respect, I don't miss him. Like his work ethic. He worked a lot harder than anyone I know. He would not take no for an answer. He would travel the world overnight to accomplish the mission, whatever it was. Or his integrity, which I admired hugely. That was why we went so far together without ever checking each other or signing formal agreements. After our first contract ended in 1975, we didn't bother signing another, as we trusted each other completely. He didn't teach me integrity because I think I had it already. But he showed me how integrity can be used in a difficult business world, and that is with me every day.

Jean-Claude Killy

> **SHORT SMART**
>
> It is very rare to find visionaries or industry leaders who are flying at 30,000 feet but still able to look down. Mark was unbelievably detailed and thorough, and prepared. Besides his drive, it is what made him great. When we took on a project, we saw how Mark did it, and thought why wouldn't we do it the same way? That approach permeated the whole organisation. We didn't have a training programme for new joiners. Our approach was, learn by being with us and watching how we do things. It was mentoring by example.
>
> *Bob Kain*

Lead by example

Frugality was important at IMG, and it came from the top. Mark didn't run the company for profit. He ploughed almost everything back into the company rather than spending it on himself. The fact was that he was building a business all his life and he never stopped in that mission. He was looking to the future and wanted to get bigger and bigger by reinvesting in the company and investing in people.

Mark's approach meant that he didn't lead the lifestyle of many of his peers. He had a lovely house, first-class travel and enjoyed good meals, but he didn't move into the area of private jets or spend lavishly on himself. Everyone in the company knew that to be the case and they respected that. He led by example. It is very hard to criticise someone on their expenses if you're flying around in a private jet. His approach also helped forge loyalty. Everyone knew that Mark was reinvesting in the business and therefore effectively reinvesting in everyone's future.

Lynton Taylor

Leave a positive footprint abroad

I have worked for IMG for over twenty years and the vast majority of that time has been spent working abroad, in places such as South Africa, Pakistan, India and Sri Lanka. I have a core team but rely heavily on freelancers, local to the area in which we are operating. Wherever we are, we have always tried to maintain our standards and practices and get people to adapt to our way of working, within our framework – while still being sensitive to the cultural differences.

IMG's culture is to be inclusive and to treat people honestly and fairly. We treat freelancers as part of the team, people who are there to contribute positively. In India, it's customary for the boss to take the credit for what has been achieved. We try to ensure that everyone has a voice.

Treating freelancers as part of the team is very important. We once had to put on an Indian Premier League (IPL) match in a new ground with just five days' notice, requiring the whole team to be put up in a hotel. We all stayed in the same hotel – from the lowest-paid worker to the highest. Each member of the team was given the same *per diem* rate. It meant that if we went out to a restaurant, we could go as a team and nobody was excluded on the basis of finances. It could mean that some of the juniors earned more on their allowance than their salary, but it was important in terms of working together.

I try to convey IMG's can-do attitude. I'm happy to pick up a paintbrush if I can see that there is something that needs patching up quickly. The reaction is one of horror – how can I possibly do that as the boss? I say: 'I can, because it will take me ten minutes to sort that bit out and you're busy doing something else. You need to understand that if I were in the UK I would be doing the same, picking up a bit of paper from the floor or whatever. I wouldn't find some junior person to do it for me.'

We also instil a tremendous work ethic and the importance of attention to detail, both strong IMG traits. I have an IPL tournament handbook and every year I give someone the task of ringing every single number in it before we publish it – there are hundreds in there. The reasons for investing time and effort in instilling the IMG culture are twofold. The more that we can raise standards, the better the pool of talent that comes back to me. A lot of the freelancers I work with want to come back and work for us again as we treat them well. IMG is so well respected everywhere. In India, we get hundreds of CVs, and I love to have anyone who has worked for IMG before working with me. I know that they will have this wonderful work ethic, and be very solid.

The second reason is opportunity. IMG gives people opportunities and if you take them and make them your own, you can grow professionally. We sold the franchises for the IPL in January and 90 days later we played our first match. In the space of that three months, we had developed the franchise regulations and sold the first franchise, had a huge player auction, and had developed all the league rules and regulations and field design for the first match. It was totally uncharted territory, but I was given the opportunity to run with it – to just get in there and do it.

What goes around comes around. I was lucky enough to have been given opportunities by IMG and I want to pass on those same opportunities to the people I work with. There are a number of people that I really believe have learned through us and have become good strong characters as a result.

Catherine Simpson

Every win and loss matters

As a big tennis fan and high-school player, I enjoyed going to Wimbledon when I was a teenager. One time that I was there, Mark came over and said, come with me, let's go for a walk. We went to one of the outside courts and watched a young Australian player who was practising with the coach Tony Roche. We sat on the side of the court watching this ball being smashed by the youngster for a minute or two before Mark said to me, 'We missed signing him – but we'll get him.'

I was struck, even then, as a young kid. I thought to myself: 'Here's Mark McCormack, who runs the biggest sports company in the world, but who is still walking around the grounds of Wimbledon, upset that he missed signing a single player. And on top of that he is going to do anything he can, including watching him practise, to sign him.' It was amazing. The easiest thing for him to do would be to shrug his shoulders and forget about it – if he even knew about it in the first place. It demonstrated to me that if you are the boss and you are running the company, there should be nothing too small for you to pay attention to or to get involved in. What's more, every win or loss matters. Mark was so focused that he knew that they had missed this one player and that upset him. Years later, I am the same. Every little win and loss I take personally and they all matter. There's no question.

Casey Wasserman

SHORT SMART

Even with English as the leading international language of business, my father strongly believed that a solid grasp of another language and a meaningful understanding of other cultures could reap huge benefits in business. He also believed that a foreign language on a CV increases your prospects of getting hired. I read French at university and the experience was life-changing. When Olympic Champion Jean-Claude Killy became president of the Organising Committee of the 1992 Olympic Winter Games, he asked IMG to run the marketing programme. IMG put a team of French speakers on secondment to the organising committee and I was lucky enough to be among them, working in the best job and for the best boss I would ever have.

Leslie McCormack Gathy

Set a clear business vision

It is a common business problem to get bogged down in the daily detail, which prevents you from seeing the bigger picture, not being able to see the wood for the trees. One of the ways Mark overcame this problem was to create a business landscape where he could see exactly what was going on.

Sports marketing was still in its infancy by the late 1970s and early 1980s, with just a handful of players in the market. IMG was dominant and had a good profile, but Mark could see the benefit of expanding that visibility across different sectors of management. It was obvious to no one but Mark that people like Kiri Te Kanawa, Jean Shrimpton and Pope John Paul II could become clients. He had created a flat landscape at IMG where all the separate divisions were visible to him and us. There were no silos or vertical structures – you could see everything that was going on. And across that flat landscape, Mark could see the synergies between the differing areas of client management and also burgeoning markets such as merchandising and licensing. So, a tennis player had the racket, shoes and clothes, but what about the watch and the car? The concept was new to the world of sport, and it was Mark who, by keeping the IMG structure open and accessible, was able to make those connections.

He could see that, just as in sport, artists and models also needed help with their endorsements, scheduling and tax returns. Even the Vatican was deeply troubled by its lack of control and structure during papal tours. IMG was used to running complex events and a multi-city papal tour was no different. It also delivered a high-quality commemorative licensing and merchandising programme, which brought value and prestige to Pope John Paul II's UK visit. Having a clear business vision with a structure that supported the company's ethos made that kind of expansion and diversification possible.

Jeremy Palmer-Tomkinson

Act ethically and sleep easy

When IMG first moved into the modelling business, it was not, in large part, a real industry. There was a lot of stuff that was questionable. But IMG was and is a company with a strong sense of ethics, one that always did the right thing. When we first opened our Paris office, all other agencies in Paris were taking cash bookings. It was the accepted norm, and it was widely considered that not paying cash to models might be a problem for them. When my boss heard about it he said: 'Well, we won't be doing that because it's illegal, and it will take me 30 seconds to explain to any one of them why they need to pay tax.' IMG did everything the right way, and it came from the top.

Mark did things with such class, and there was reassurance in knowing things were being done properly. You could put your head on the pillow at night and know that you had acted the right way, that you followed through, and that you were a woman of your word. His level of ethics in business was pretty astonishing. There are many titans of business who seem to lose some of their values along the way. I remember going to restaurants with my dad and if the waiters were rude or arrogant, he would always say the owner is probably a nightmare. It always comes from the top. You don't have bad staff if you are a great boss.

Because Mark was such an ethical person, it filtered through the company, and still does. All of the senior people at IMG Models have been here for twenty years and worked under him. His ethical approach is evident in everything we do. It's a driver for us all, and an important part of our success.

Jeni Rose

Don't forget the greater good

Some people try to demonstrate their philosophically under-pinned approach to sport by decrying sponsorship and saying that sport will never be the same with commercial influences. These tend to be the people who have never wondered where their next meal is coming from.

By achieving what he did for athletes, Mark often freed three or four generations of a family from financial fragility. Of course, there is a balance of judgement. We are all familiar with the saying, 'he who pays the piper calls the tune'. We certainly don't want the people paying the piper rewriting the symphony, but we often overlook the fact that people like Mark changed the lives of individuals and families. Business is business, but, with the right kind of ethos, business can and must be a force for good.

Sebastian Coe

In times of growth, keep things simple

During my time at IMG we were the market leader in an industry that was growing at a phenomenal pace. With so much going on, keeping track could have been overwhelming. In terms of finance, Mark's way of coping was to distil complex things into simple elements.

Businesses go in phases. When we were growing, top-line revenue growth while managing the increase in costs was more important than profitability of individual business areas. As time went on, we looked more at net profitability but, during that period of phenomenal growth, doing so would have nega-tively impacted the entrepreneurial culture of the company. We were managed on revenue growth and none of the people running those businesses really had an idea of the costs involved. The finance team generated a bi-monthly report of the income projections for each individual client. Mark reviewed this in great detail. Memos would go out checking minor details, keeping everybody on their toes and motivating people to keep growing each of our various businesses.

Mark managed costs mainly by headcount, which was a very

simple measure. I discovered this when I was sent to run our office in Monaco. After about a month, I noticed that one of our clients who lived in Monaco but was away a lot would have items delivered to the office. It was a constant distraction having to deal with these deliveries, so I decided to hire a part-time receptionist. It seemed a trivial $10k decision.

During a monthly catch-up with my boss, I mentioned, in passing, that I was hiring a part-time receptionist. He said that he was pleased I had mentioned it. He had a meeting coming up with Mark to discuss headcount, so could I write him a memo, and based on what I had said, he was pretty sure that the decision to hire could be approved. Besides being extremely glad I had brought it up, I went away thinking what an insight it was into how the business was managed. It seemed very strange that the owner and chairman of the company would be involved in a decision over me hiring a part-time receptionist. I was making many more significant decisions, but headcount was the major driver of our cost base. Mark knew that if he could control the growth in headcount, he could control the growth in the costs of the whole business. It was very simple. Drive the top line, focusing hard on how much we are making from every activity, and just manage costs by keeping control of headcount.

It did lead to some issues. The focus on additions to headcount meant that we did not systematically review past headcount decisions. But it was a very simple way of managing the business, allowing Mark to spend his time on where the real value was. The lesson to learn was the benefit in distilling complicated things into simple metrics. The information will not be perfect but in a fast-growing business it is better to be 80 per cent right quickly than 100 per cent right and take months to get to the decision.

Peter Griffiths

Manage your own growth

The bigger the company gets the further you can be from the decision makers. I am lucky in that I have been at IMG a long time. I have worked with my boss, the global head of tennis, for 25 years, and although he is in Barcelona, we've been in the trenches together, which makes it easy for me to pick up the phone. He is involved in the development of our London team but, given his location, doesn't have such ready contact with them. They are a young team who work on two events in London. But as their experience grows, we want them to grow. I try to broker the opportunities for them to work on other events abroad. If I recommend people to my colleagues, they will listen, but those people need to get in front of them, have a chat with them, and try to make that personal connection. That is why I encourage my team every year to go to the IMG hospitality house during Wimbledon.

I say to staff: you might not have a specific role but make a point to get there anyway. You will be welcome and you will get to know people in different divisions, and more importantly get to know the global leaders in the tennis division in a more relaxed setting. If they take charge of building those relationships themselves, they will be much better placed to grab hold of any opportunities that may arise. Growing a business is also about growing the people in it, and encouraging them to play an active role in their own development can make all the difference.

Jan Felgate

Never stop learning

Business constantly evolves and we are on a lifelong journey of learning. I probably spend a day a month on my own professional development, even at this stage in my career. I find that the more I know, the less I know. Business is changing, competition is increasing, and technology is disrupting. These are central themes for all businesses today. To be relevant in five years' time, we need to constantly question our practices and policies and how we do business, something that Mark did throughout his career.

I have a holistic approach to learning. I read trade journals, and go to seminars. I am part of a network of young presidents and world presidents. It is a global organisation and we meet monthly. It is a safe place to go and talk about opportunities and issues you have when you are in a leadership position. When you are inside an organisation, people don't necessarily tell you all the things you should hear or want to hear. Having outside counsel is very helpful.

I also tend to look outside the sports world to see how other brands are building their business, an IMG trait I learned from my boss. He would throw down a newspaper clipping of some company, saying they are doing this, find out who the decision maker is and let's get a meeting to see if we can do a deal. There is no need to be myopic and keep your focus within your industry. Lessons can be learned anywhere.

Stacey Allaster

Reinforce messages

After I had been at IMG for a year or two, I got a call to say that Mark wanted to meet me. When I asked what it was about I was told nothing specific, which immediately put me on edge – that was not the usual modus operandi of the company. When we met, Mark pulled out a number of different receipts that I had submitted as expenses. He went through them and then asked how much I left as a tip. I said 20 per cent.

'Always?' he queried.

'Yes. Why? I thought that was what you are meant to tip.'

'I tip between 15 and 20 per cent,' Mark countered. 'I will

only tip 20 per cent if I think I have been given the best possible service by the waiter.'

'If it makes any difference I tip 20 per cent all the time, not just on work-related items.'

'Not really. Just go back to 15–20 per cent in business,' he concluded.

Mark had not arranged that meeting just to talk about those specific expenses and how much I should tip when I next took a cab. It was to show that he was aware of detail and that everything that the company did mattered, down to the smallest particular of how much you tip. It kept you on your toes to know that the owner of the company would be paying that level of attention to the smallest areas of the business, and made sure you followed suit. But it was also a lesson about service. It was about the fact that we are in a service industry and we would expect to be paid for the service we deliver. In order for us to be paid well, that service needs to be the very best that it can be, and our clients extremely satisfied.

Gavin Forbes

SHORT SMART

The first McCormack business tip I read in Mark's *Success Secrets* newsletter related to paper clips. Mark said that every day he was mailed something with a paper clip attached. He realised that if he took that paper clip off and put it in a dish on his desk, he would never need to buy paper clips again. It made me laugh to think that he would even think about such a small thing, let alone write it. But to this day, before I throw any bit of paper in the bin, I take the paper clip off and put it in a dish on my desk. I have been here for 25 years and never bought paper clips. And I think of him every time, thinking how happy he would be.

Jeni Rose

Make your presence felt

I once met Mark for drinks at the French Open, in his hotel room. At the time, he was having his annual meeting with his French team discussing budgets and the like. The hotel room was a twin room, with one chair. He was sitting on the end of one of the beds overseeing a budget discussion. It clearly made everyone uncomfortable to have their chairman perched on the end of a single bed, and they kept offering Mark the chair, but he would refuse, saying that he was fine where he was.

It was a brilliant ploy. Firstly, it was very difficult to get financially expansive about budgets if your boss is sitting on the end of a bed, which made for a very focused discussion. Secondly, what better way to demonstrate the level of frugality that Mark expected from his staff than to hold an annual meeting in his own somewhat understated twin room. He made his presence felt, and also reinforced messages about budgetary restraint.

David Gilmour

Take a snapshot of corporate health

When I first started working at IMG in a very junior position, one of my jobs was to monitor faxes coming in and out of the London office. Pre-email, a lot of correspondence was conducted via fax. Every fax that went in and out of the London office was delivered to Mark's office every day. My job was to flick through them and to pull out anything that I thought was of interest. That might be new business, or perhaps something that didn't look like it was going as smoothly as it should, or where the tone was hostile. I would get a stack of faxes to flick through each day and I would pull out six or so.

By looking at a selection of these faxes, Mark had an overview of what was going on in the office. With the advent of email, a central 'File Centre' account was created for the same purpose.

Employees were instructed to cc the File Centre on all external emails, again so that Mark could keep his finger on the pulse of what was happening. It was his way of taking a snapshot, keeping a track on what was really happening day to day, rather than relying on what he was being told.

Catherine Simpson

Know when to pull the plug

Every once in a while, Mark got burned. He was enamoured with a musical that one of his clients had written, called *American Heroes*. He agreed to produce it and then persuaded John DeLorean to underwrite it. It was to start in the West End and then go to Broadway. We were in the US preparing the show when DeLorean ran into difficulties, leaving Mark on the hook financially.

We went around trying to raise money for the musical. For months I worked incredibly hard trying to raise money from investor groups in different locations. It was fascinating but all the while Mark was teaching me that you have to separate the emotion from the business side. Emotionally we so wanted it to happen and had invested a lot of time in trying. We did a workshop that went extraordinarily well but unfortunately didn't get any offers from big Broadway theatres, only an off-Broadway venue. The economics were such that it cost us more to run the show each week than we could have made, given the size of the theatre.

When it came to it, Mark made the smarter, but harder, business decision and shut it down. It demonstrated that while emotion helps generate creativity and new projects, you must still be able to make the business call at any point.

One other point was that there was no blame game afterwards. Mark was practical and realistic. He didn't like to lose at anything and was the most competitive person ever, but there were no recriminations, despite this definitely being a loss. Sometimes in business you need to know when to pull the plug, no matter how much you've invested – both emotionally and financially – in a project or new venture. Failure is, unfortunately, just part of business. The trick is to learn from that failure and move on as cleanly as possible.

Howard Katz

8

Joining the dots

*... start with the best; learn from the best; expand
slowly and solidify ... then horizontally diversify.*

Not everyone will agree with MHM's personal approach to
growing a business, as Sir Martin Sorrell reminds us in chapter
7. The key thing is to find the strategies for growth that will
work for you, your business philosophy and the markets in
which you're operating. But there is much we can *all* learn from
MHM's focus on connectivity, collaboration and planning.
Business growth is often about the right combinations of factors
or 'connections'. Chapter 8 offers examples aplenty of how to
join the dots, whether by thinking laterally, using data and
information creatively or collaborating with colleagues and
peers.

Readers of a certain age may remember the hit television
franchise, *Superstars*, which pitted athletes from different sports
against each other in a series of sporting challenges. Dick Alford
tells the story of how IMG was able to connect its sponsorship
contacts and production capabilities with its relationships with
athletes to make the show happen – joining the dots in the most
creative way possible.

This is a prime example of horizontal diversification, the
ability to use existing business experience and relationships to
expand into new, but related, fields. It's a strategy used to great
effect by MHM and IMG. Breck McCormack recalls how his

father was always looking to take ideas that worked in one place and duplicate them somewhere else, whether that meant moving into another sport or expanding internationally. Wherever possible, **take your existing experience and expertise into new markets rather than reinventing the wheel**. Vertical diversification into new areas where you have much less of a foothold can be much riskier.

Collaboration and partnerships are also powerful growth strategies, especially if resources are tight, or if you want to take advantage of a partner's expertise or market access. Indoor tennis events were unheard of, let alone at the Albert Hall, but, on the back of collaboration on the World Match Play golf tournament, explains George Hammond, Rothmans was persuaded to branch into sponsorship of a new area. For Hammond, this was an example of how MHM's vision and foresight was able to bring parties together to develop the sports industry as a whole. The same is true for business partnerships. Breck McCormack reminds us that, under the right conditions, **sharing ownership and splitting the proceeds can be a positive way forward** as well as a compromise.

According to Tony Godsick, making the right connections doesn't just mean meeting the right people; it also means listening to them, processing what they're telling you and connecting all this with new business opportunities. To make the most of horizontal diversification, **match the right contact with the right new opportunity**, preferably at an opportune time. Making the most of these kinds of connections, however, requires planning, preparation and using as much insight as you can muster. Alastair Johnston is clear that IMG's access to data helped them secure business, especially in the early days of sports management when there were very few hard and fast industry norms or standards. Planning can also give you the insight you need to hold fire on expansion, as witnessed by IMG's Operation Cape Horn. **Information really is power**; use and analyse all of the data you have to hand in order to get ahead. Look for patterns and trends that will guide your action. And, if all else fails, don't be afraid to ask for advice from a trusted contact.

Collaboration for growth can also be successfully harnessed internally. Gary Swain proves that encouraging staff themselves to diversify horizontally can be good for both business and personal growth. Involve staff in policy-making, use peer review to manage risk, and make sure that staff are engaged with the numbers, especially cash flow and profitability. It all helps to join the dots.

Piece the picture together

I left IMG for a while and went to work for Dick Button, the twice-Olympic figure-skating champion, at Candid Productions. Dick came up with an idea for a show that would determine the world's greatest athlete: it was to be called *Superstars*. He pitched the idea to Barry Frank at TWI [the TV production arm of IMG, now IMG Media] over lunch one day, and Barry could see the potential. At that time, the TV networks wouldn't take anything on unless it came with sponsorship. IMG had a network of sponsorship contacts to tap into, and Barry's next stop was Fram Oil Filters who were looking to get more heavily involved in sports and who duly came on board. Armed with a sponsor, Barry headed over to ABC television, where the relationship was well established. He was told that it was a good and innovative idea, but that there was no way the top athletes would agree to it, as they wouldn't want to be seen losing to their peers.

Barry's response was to write up a list of the 25 greatest athletes in the world at that time. He said to ABC, 'If I can get ten of the people on that list to appear, will you agree to air it?' ABC, who had lost the rights to show national basketball association games and had a gap in their winter schedule, were prepared to give it a go. With concept, production (through TWI), sponsor and network in the bag, the athletes would not be a problem. Of the ten competitors originally scheduled to compete, practically all were IMG clients.

When the show was first aired, it proved to be an instant success, and was quickly developed into a franchise, spawning international versions and team events. It was a classic example of the power of being able to piece the picture together. Expansion of IMG interests into diverse but related areas meant that deals that might otherwise seem impossible were achievable.

Dick Alford

No need to reinvent the wheel

My father was always looking for an opportunity to take ideas that worked in one place and duplicate them somewhere else. His original success came from representing professional golfers, but he soon moved on to representing tennis players, and eventually athletes from almost every sport in the world. Likewise, once his business was up and running successfully in the US, he began thinking about how he could expand internationally.

I travelled with my father extensively while I was running the IMG business in Asia. Given his reputation, we were able to set up numerous meetings at the very highest levels when we travelled to new territories like India, China, Thailand or Korea. Quite often at these meetings, there would be an agenda, such as the need to sell sponsorship for a major event coming up in the country in question. But far more often, he would come to the meeting with an open mind, ready to 'listen aggressively'. Normally, he would have a number of ideas in mind, but he wouldn't lead by presenting them. They would be like arrows in his quiver, to be pulled out seemingly as a spontaneous suggestion if the other party raised a goal or a priority where one of these ideas might genuinely help. More often than not, the basis of these 'new' ideas would be an event or concept that had worked beautifully in another market, but had not yet been tried in the emerging market we were visiting.

I have seen this strategy impress more than one potential customer, and it is something I have tried to use myself, and indeed tried to get our whole sales team to use. At our annual Asian meetings, one of our main tasks was to brainstorm possible new events for each market using our existing knowledge. We created expenses budgets for various ideas, which helped to establish how much money we would need from a title sponsor in order to launch profitably. This preparation enabled us to come up with a 'spontaneous' idea, complete with cost estimates and potential dates, once we heard a customer describe goals and objectives that might well be achieved by what we were ready to propose. Not only did it impress, but it also allowed us to move to the next stage quickly. Using existing experience and not having to reinvent the wheel every time gave us an important competitive edge.

Breck McCormack

Think laterally

For my first nine years at IMG, I was based in Cleveland. I was starting to think about my future and what I should do next – my thought was to return to Dallas and open IMG's first office there. I put the suggestion to my boss, Bob Kain, who asked me to put together a business plan. I did that and waited to hear about next steps. Sometime later we were at Wimbledon and at 7 p.m. one night, Bob said, 'Do you have your business plan together, because we are meeting Mark at 10 a. m. tomorrow and he would like to hear it.'

So I stayed up that night and went through the plan carefully. I walked into the room the next day and the first thing Mark said was, 'why Dallas?' I explained that I had grown up around there, and worked my first seven years in sports management in Dallas. I had a lot of contacts, and the Southwest region was a great market for IMG business development. He said: 'What do you think about Chicago?' When I replied, 'why Chicago?', he continued, saying: 'Well, it's a bigger city, we already have an IMG office there, and there are events that you can oversee, including the Ameritech Cup, which is a WTA Tour event. What do you think?' I said, 'Chicago it is.'

Mark was always thinking one or two steps ahead of you. He was thinking about what was best for me, and how best to keep me successful at IMG. He took what I wanted to do and figured out the best opportunity for IMG to make it happen. He knew that I produced events, in addition to representing clients, and I wouldn't have been able to do that as easily in a new office with less support. I hadn't thought about Chicago, but it ended up being a much better opportunity for me.

The role I took when I first joined IMG was not something I expected to be doing. I had been working for a sports management firm in Dallas. Between 1981 and 1986 I produced, promoted and staged the John McEnroe Tennis over America tours, which consisted of 99 one-night exhibitions in 90 US cities. I had also managed NBA Basketball Tours and other professional tennis tours, so I was asked if I could produce a figure-skating tour.

I knew very little about figure skating, but IMG represented Dorothy Hamill and Scott Hamilton, both of whom were Olympic gold medallists. Scott had recently completed a contract with Ice Capades, but was dissatisfied with having to skate with cartoon characters, Smurfs and plumes. Bob Kain, who headed up the IMG Winter Sport Division, had the vision, along with Scott, to create a show that would be similar to a Broadway production, with amazing lights and great music and choreography. Bob convinced me that there was huge potential and that with the necessary support and funding, and my experience, IMG would make the tour a reality. I joined IMG in 1986 and later that year we produced our first Stars On Ice tour. Thirty years later it's still going. As co-executive producer, I had the opportunity to be a part of something truly amazing that I would never have thought of. It was a question of IMG seeing your potential and developing you in areas that you would not have considered, thinking laterally to develop both the business and the people working in it.

Gary Swain

The power of collaboration

If you have the vision but not the resources to grow a company, collaboration can be of significant benefit.

In the years before cigarette advertising was banned, tobacco companies were at the forefront of sports sponsorship with seemingly limitless budgets. I was asked by my chairman at the British tobacco company Rothmans to organise a golf tournament, something I had not done before. The tournament went off without a hitch and not long after, Mark, who had his client Jack Nicklaus playing at the event, came over to meet me.

He suggested that as the tournament had gone well, Rothmans should organise a match play, as that was the favourite form of golf in England. I replied that there already was one, the News of the World Match Play. No, he corrected, I mean a *world* match play and I will guarantee Arnold Palmer, Gary Player and Jack Nicklaus to play at it. There were not many European players at that time, and no American golfers came to the UK, so the idea was exciting. My chairman readily agreed, I found Wentworth as a venue, and the World Match Play was born.

We formed a committee with representative members from the R&A, United States Golf Association, and Mark. He would put forward suggestions and ideas as to how the event could work and I always listened to what he said. Mark saw it as a world event and came up with the concept of an eight-man field, with invitations going to the winners of the majors. Because Mark had devised it and both Arnold and Gary thought it was a great event, the aura of the tournament spread among the professionals. Every professional wanted an invitation and its prestige grew. The players were flown over first class, stayed in the river suites along the Thames at the Savoy, and had chauffeur-driven Daimler cars to take them to the tournament. It all added to the event's reputation, which from the outset was a huge success.

When I left Rothmans in 1977, the tournament was not going to be kept on by the company as we had a new CEO who did not like sponsorships of any kind. I said to Mark 'the tournament should be yours', and at that point, now that IMG had its own events division, they took it over. Initially, Mark got Colgate to sponsor it and then found Suntory whisky. He was big enough and respected enough by then to be able to talk directly to CEOs about sponsorship.

Much the same happened with tennis. We were not sponsoring tennis at all, but Mark suggested that we put on an event in London. When I replied that there wasn't anywhere other than Wimbledon, he said why don't you go indoors, before adding, flippantly, why not the Albert Hall? He said its appeal should be as an event for the old stars, not for the youngsters who would be playing at Wimbledon. Indoor tennis was unheard of in the UK, but we looked into it and decided to go ahead. The event became Rothmans Indoor Tennis, now Champions Tennis, and although IMG was not involved in the organisation, they were again able to provide some of the top former champion players, like Rod Laver. When we gave up the event, no money changed hands; it was just a logical step for it to go to Mark.

Mark could see that, across the industry, collaboration would be to everyone's benefit. He was responsible for improving relations between sporting bodies and television companies. He made sure that everyone was happy and he played a huge role in keeping the disparate elements together for the greater good of all. Mark could see the advantage to sport of having the widest possible television coverage. As far back as the seventies, before Sky was on the scene, Mark suggested to the BBC head of outside broadcasts that the BBC should set up a dedicated sports channel. He thought it was a good idea but it was rejected by his bosses who said that it would never work. If the BBC had had a dedicated sports channel, Sky, as we know it, would not exist. Mark had vision and foresight, and wanted to bring everyone with him to help increase the size of the playing field. That kind of creative and collaborative thinking was the basis of IMG's success, and is a model for how all sorts of organisations can grow.

George Hammond

Sometimes two parties are better than one

My father always stressed the business potential of events. As he would say, Bjorn Borg might break a leg, but Wimbledon cannot. Representing an event was a good step forward, but it was not total control and could be taken away. That's why my father wanted to create and build IMG's own golf events like the World Match Play Championship or the Dunhill Cup. IMG was ideally placed to do so given our client base, our television arm, and good relationships with potential sponsors.

The ideal scenario was to have a title sponsor in place that would more than cover expenses. But we also looked to own events in partnership with governing bodies. When I drafted the agreement between IMG and the European PGA Tour, my father stressed that it must be drafted in a way that made us partners forever. We might lose money in the early years, but he was sure being partners on the most important golf tour outside of the US PGA Tour would be invaluable in the future. Needless to say, he was right.

Another variation was to form a partnership with the title sponsor of the event. Normally, an event is only profitable if there is a good title sponsorship agreement in place. However, the secondary sponsors often make a significant contribution towards profits, and sometimes there is tension between the wishes of the title sponsor and the secondary sponsors. One way to reduce this tension was to make the title sponsor our partner on the event. We would share with them the event budget, including a reasonable fee for ourselves to cover overheads. But we would then share the income from secondary sponsors. This way our interests were fully aligned. In some cases, being prepared to share ownership and business proceeds is a positive step forward rather than a compromise.

Breck McCormack

Commit to the long term

The biggest thing I took into my business life beyond IMG was how to sign up sponsors. At IMG I once bumped into Mark in the corridor and he asked me how I was getting on with finding new sponsors for various events. I replied that things were going really well and that we were on a bit of a roll. He said: 'That's fantastic, but always remember that the easiest part of this business is getting a sponsor. The more difficult part is keeping a sponsor. Once you have had the meetings, done the negotiations, and secured the sponsorship, don't then just send invoices out. You have got to manage that sponsor's expectations, be in regular contact, and make them feel that they have made the right decision.'

He was right. So often it's easy to get the deal done; it's keeping the deal that takes more work and effort. It is something I say regularly to my young executives. I tell them to draw up a calendar of dates on which they will make contact, because if it's not written down, it won't happen. It may be that when the day comes to ring that particular sponsor you might be ringing with nothing to say, but you still call and say, 'I just wanted to check in with you and see if everything's OK.' Something that basic makes all the difference. It's worth going above and beyond and thinking outside the box to see if there is something that will appeal. Ring up on the off-chance with a suggestion: 'I've got this

idea that I just wanted to run past you. It may not be for you, but
…' It shows that you are working hard for them, and thinking
about them beyond the confines of the contract.

After big events it takes no effort to send flowers or choco-
lates, or a thank-you letter, to all the people at the sponsoring
company who have actually put in the work at their end in order
to make it happen. And I also send out framed photos of the day,
or perhaps a little photo album made up for the boss of the sponsoring company. It is straight out of the McCormack handbook,
and it is so effective. Keeping business relationships going long
term takes commitment, attention to detail and a determination
to find new ways to keep the relationship going.

Neil Hobday

Make the connections

Mark would often take pictures of people at an event, even if
he had only just been introduced to them, and send them onto
them afterwards. He told me that he did it because it would act
as a nice memory of a good time, and it was also a nice gesture.
But the pictures were also sent to people in their offices, and he
knew that when they got that picture, they would put it in their
desk. It was his hope that when they opened their desk drawer,
they would see it and think, do you know what, I haven't spoken
to Mark since we were at that event. What a great guy. I'm going
to call him and do some business.

Whenever you called Mark, there was always an invite to
some event and something would flow from that. He was very
good at bringing influential business people into his world. He
invented corporate hospitality. He was the architect and creator
of the whole thing and used it to full advantage. He brought
so many people into his world – clients, business people from
diverse industries, politicians, people from differing sports,
sponsors. It was genius.

He found a way with whomever he met to elicit some sort of nugget of information, which led to an opportunity to do business with them. He was good at enquiring about things in a gentle way and asking questions, and then processing during the conversation how the information he was receiving could be used for other parts of the business somewhere else in the world. I have taken that skill away. Thanks to my time at IMG, I have so many strong relationships with people around the world. When I meet people, I listen to everything that they say and process it and store it. I might not be able to use it right away, but it could lead to business down the line. Making the right connections doesn't just mean meeting the right people; it also means listening to them, processing what they're telling you and connecting all this with new business opportunities.

Tony Godsick

SHORT SMART

My boss once asked me to give a one-sentence summary of what he should do in a certain situation. I struggled so hard to do it and spent ages trying to work out what to put, only to end up with an eight-line paragraph that was one sentence. It was a real lesson into the importance of being concise and to the point. The ability to see through to what is the core issue and articulate that in an accurate and concise way, and bring clarity to an area where none exists, is a real skill, which I then trained myself to do.

Timo Lumme

Keep your competitors close

I set up ProServ in 1970, initially to represent tennis players such as Arthur Ashe and Stan Smith. At the time, IMG was focused on golfers and we were not direct competitors, but as our businesses grew there was increasing overlap. Mark and I called ourselves 'friendly competitors'. We used to meet secretly twice a year. The idea behind the meetings was to establish that we could compete with each other but that there were certain ethical guidelines that would shape our behaviour. It was very helpful to have that understanding and it set a good tone. It meant that Mark and I treated each other differently to other competitors that subsequently came into the field. It also enabled us to work together on a major lawsuit that had huge ramifications for our industry.

The lawsuit was with the Men's International Professional Tennis Council (MIPTC). The council was the forerunner to the ATP board today and effectively ran pro tennis. Volvo was a client of ProServ who thought that they were being discriminated against by the MIPTC and were suing for the loss of their sponsorship of the men's pro circuit. But the battle became more of a power play, with the MIPTC increasingly alarmed by the role that agents played in representing players, events and television properties.

I flew to Norfolk, Virginia to meet Mark at the airport. Mark got off his plane and said to me, 'I've got nineteen minutes before I've got to get my connecting flight.' So I said: 'Mark, here's the picture. We're suing the men's pro council. They're trying to push the agents out. They are going to try to force the issue, and say that if you represent talent you can't represent events as well. I think we should join forces in the lawsuit so that we are twice as strong. It's going to be a huge anti-trust case that will take a long time and be very expensive.' He asked me a couple of questions and then said: 'I'll join you in the suit. We'll split the attorney fees, we'll use your anti-trust law firm in Washington, but on one condition. You don't see the memos in my file and I don't see yours. We keep them and our businesses separate.' I readily agreed.

And in that nineteen minutes it was done. It was a big move and a momentous meeting. The parties joined as plaintiffs together and were then countersued by the MIPTC who accused us of 'exert[ing] extensive power over players from the cradle to the grave.'

The case went to court and was initially thrown out, but several years later we won the appeal. It was a gigantic win in tennis that enabled agents to operate in the way they do today. If we hadn't won, our business would have been cut in half. And without the ability to work together, despite being competitors, who knows what the result might have been.

Donald Dell

The personal touch

In 1992, I was in charge of the IMG Brussels office, which was very small. Mark was invited to come and speak at a conference in town. He called me to say that he was coming, and that he intended to spend a day or two with me, so I should organise his time. I arranged a series of half-hour meetings with chairmen and CEOs of businesses in Brussels. It was fantastic for me to have the door opened at the very top tier by these people who were happy to welcome Mark into their office. It saved a lot of time being able to go straight in at that level, rather than working up, which I would have had to do on my own. One of the meetings was with the CEO of DHL International. We were at the renowned restaurant, La Truffe Noire, so we had a relaxed 90 minutes, chatting in an informal atmosphere. I could sense that something had changed compared with previous meetings, and I decided to seize the moment and pitch an idea. Tennis player Jim Courier had just turned number one in the world, so I suggested that it would be great for DHL, as the number one courier company in the world, to have Courier, the number one tennis player, as their ambassador. We can communicate around that – sponsorships, endorsements, personal appearances and hospitality, I enthused. The CEO turned to me and said, 'I like the idea, but between you and me, we are not a courier company.' At which point Mark burst out laughing, and in that instant, a relationship had been formed. It was illustrative to me. We continued to have a very good and long relationship both with Courier and DHL, but without that special time, the dinner, maybe we wouldn't have done the deal.

I saw that, if and when you do business internationally, you do not get customers from sitting behind your computer. You need to create those special moments. I needed to get out more. Now I spend 200 days on the road. I plan in advance, thinking 'who can I have lunch with?' I call our local offices and ask them to set up meetings in the same way that Mark did with me. I'm always looking to create that special moment.

When I meet my sales team, my questions are always, 'Who have you met this month? How will you grow the business by selling the same product to the same people?' You need to find new products and new customers. And you do that by getting out there, meeting people and building relationships. The world of email and social media has made connecting with people much easier, but there's still no substitute for the personal touch.

Michel Masquelier

Planning matters

In the early 1990s Mark, along with many chief executives, was wrestling with the idea of expansion into Latin America. Understanding how to do business and make inroads into the continent, with its untapped potential, was an enigma for businesses. Mark's approach was Operation Cape Horn.

Three or four IMG executives were assembled together, and

over six months, planned a simultaneous country-by-country assault of the region. Each country would be visited for three weeks by either one person or a small team. I was part of a team of three assigned to Mexico. Our role was to meet with people of interest to establish what opportunities might exist. Meetings were set up for us every day for three weeks, arranged by reaching out to existing clients and IMG customers and asking for their help in the form of an introduction to their Latin American colleagues. Our existing network was fascinated with the project and couldn't have been more forthcoming. The planning was meticulous and every hour of my time for that three-week period, even down to restaurant bookings, was accounted for. We had briefing notes to read prior to each meeting, and we then had to show up, be adaptive, interested, and write detailed reports on the opportunities available. It was an amazing undertaking, spanning every country in the region, from Bolivia to Brazil.

Ultimately, the decision at that time was that there was not enough low-hanging fruit to justify opening offices across the continent. In Mexico, Brazil and Argentina, we found some people in companies with whom we decided to stay in very close contact, and we proceeded with opportunities on a selective basis. We wouldn't have known how to do that without Cape Horn. Rather than opening offices in what we assumed would be growth areas for us, this focused approach saved IMG millions, not to mention savings in terms of time and effort. The two key benefits were to know where to focus, and, equally, to know where not to focus. In terms of optimisation of scarce resources – time and money – it was brilliant. It proved that investment in meticulous planning up front would be paid back in spades.

Andy Pierce

> **SHORT SMART**
>
> I was once told by an important business leader that I should
> smile more. This deceptively simple piece of advice was quite
> serious. He said that if he walked out of a meeting with a frown,
> his share price could plummet. I now try to smile as much as
> I can, even when I'm worried. To be upbeat and positive and
> let people know that I love my job is simply my responsibility
> as a leader, and while I don't always succeed, this is a really
> important lesson.
>
> *Jim Kim*

Information is power

The reason we managed to grow IMG to the size that we did was
fundamentally a function of the fact that we had access to more
data. We were streets ahead of our competitors, and the more
big clients we had, the more we could accurately predict costs
and revenue expectations. That gave us a huge advantage going
into any negotiations. Businesses have to learn how to cost their
product, but in the newly formed world of sports marketing,
there was no manual that would helpfully say at what price to
pitch a particular deal. It came down to experience, and the more
deals we did, the better able we were to price them in a way that
was realistic and fair, for both us and the other party. People
who tried to compete with us were paranoid about under- or
overvaluing their client, thereby not getting the best deal. We
could price effectively.

This use of data was used to great effect when Tiger Woods
turned pro in 1996. We negotiated a big deal with Nike. We had
tennis clients who had contracts with the company and from
prior dealings with them we were well aware of how much they
wanted to move into the golf arena. A deal with Tiger would
give them immediate high-profile access, compared with having

to spend time, cost and effort in developing golf equipment that would give them credibility in the market. They knew that Tiger was the best player in the world, and were prepared to pay a significant sum for that instant brand recognition. We knew full well how much it meant to them and what would be a realistic sum in the circumstances.

Keenly aware of the power of information, in our early days every piece of correspondence had to be copied to Mark. He was also determined that our information would not fall into the wrong hands. I had to see that risk mitigated and was engaged in some ways as his corporate sleuth. While minutes of meetings had to be copied and distributed to numerous people, we developed a formula that meant that there was a very small variation within each copy. If there were a leak outside the company, it would be traceable.

It was an extreme and slightly paranoid measure, but it reflected a certain point in the company's development. When we first started, information was king, and the key factor in keeping us a step ahead. As the company grew, so too did Mark's confidence and understanding that he had to trust people and be inclusive rather than exclusive. It was part of the learning curve and an important step in building IMG.

Alastair Johnston

SHORT SMART

Never talk about business in a public elevator: that was Mark's top tip to me. 'You never know who the other people around you are. I can't tell you how much stuff I have heard about my own company in an elevator,' he remarked.

Dick Alford

Be prepared

There is an Abraham Lincoln quote that goes, if I am given six hours to chop down a tree I will spend four of them sharpening up the axe. I love that quote because it is all about preparation and thinking ahead. It stood me in good stead when dealing with Mark.

Mark used to get up early in the morning to read documents and make phone calls. It became habitual that he would look at all the scores and results that came through on a Sunday night and the impact that they had on the world rankings. I would come in rather less early than he did, to my desk in London, and I would get a call at about 9 a.m., which was 4 a.m. for Mark in the US. He would dispense with pleasantries and go straight in with: 'When so and so client came eighth in the Swiss Masters, where did that move him to in the world rankings and is that the highest ranking he has had?'

He would have read all these statistics and results overnight and have questions that he wanted answered. It's worth noting that, even in pre-internet days, without Google or tournament websites, Mark still managed to glean the information he needed from newspapers and television. I remember all too clearly the first of those Monday morning calls he made. Although I was working in the front line of golf, I think he had the better of me on each of the first four questions. One experience was enough. From then on I would make sure that I had the stats on Sunday night and be in early on Monday morning, ready for the call. I was always slightly disappointed if then he didn't ring.

For me it was a very good lesson in how I did my work. I learned that the only way that I can be as prepared as I would like to be is by getting up early. I now get up at 5 a.m. and it gives me over two hours when I can catch up, read stuff, and be ready for the day. I can then have breakfast with the family before going into the office. I was not a morning person before, but I have found it invaluable, particularly in the role I have now, which means that I deal with Asia, US and Europe. And I now expect the same levels of preparedness from those around me. If my people are not prepared for a meeting, I will, for sure, come down hard on them.

Guy Kinnings

SHORT SMART

Gary Player used to say, 'The harder I work, the luckier I get.' It was also one of my grandfather's favourite quotes. Having signed Palmer, Player and Nicklaus as his first clients, he was the first to admit the role that luck played in launching IMG. However, he also prided himself on working harder than anyone at IMG. He once told me that he liked getting up at 4 a.m. and calling executives in the London office. After being told that they hadn't yet arrived, he took a special delight in leaving a message asking them to call back, giving them his phone number in New York.

Chris McCormack

Find the right advice when you need it

Nothing can beat experience. If you find yourself in uncharted territory, asking advice from someone who has been there before will be more effective than trying to battle through on your own.

As we moved into 2002, IMG was under pressure from its bankers. The company had bought into the Indian Wells tennis tournament and was heavily involved in the construction of a new tennis stadium. It had also bought New York Fashion Week, but had had to cancel the event because of the tragedy of the 9/11 attacks. Cash that was supposed to flow in from a successful event was flowing in the other direction. Mark ran the business to extend its international reach and market dominance rather than make money, and used bank borrowing to do so. The bankers had been happy with that situation until the end of 2001, but now they wanted IMG to repay its loans. How to react?

The bankers thought that by declaring a technical default in the loan agreements they could force IMG into some form of recapitalisation – perhaps payment in shares from the existing shareholders – that would make them 'comfortable'. Mark was not about to agree to anything like that. However, just like the rest of us, he had no experience in dealing with unhappy bankers.

In the midst of this pressure, Mark invited me to lunch with Herb Siegel. At the time, I had no idea what he had in mind. I knew that Herb had been successful in taking Chris-Craft Industries from a recreational boat-building business to a media empire. I wondered if, somehow, Mark might be talking to Herb about investing in IMG. That was the furthest thing from his mind. He knew that Herb had experience of our situation with the banks, and he wanted to know how to go about dealing with them.

Mark asked me to recount IMG's current situation. I described the fifteen-member bank group, the reliance we had on cash for operations, our diverse global business and its resilience, but the unease of the bankers and the problems that that could cause with IMG's operations.

Herb listened carefully. He said that we'd be in for a tough time. The bankers would press us in every way they could. But, he observed, the only way they had a hope of being repaid was if IMG continued to operate effectively. Herb told me to listen carefully to the bankers in the meetings and to respond as well and as helpfully as possible. Then, when the demands became impossible, simply push back my chair and look at my shoes. We were in a tough situation, but we could only do what we could, no more.

This was inspired advice. It was a counsel to stick to my guns and not be forced into something to which we were fundamentally opposed, and from someone who had successful experience in a similar situation. In my dealings with Mark, he always found an answer – in this case from his connections, who were always both experienced and smart. The result of applying Herb's advice was to buy enough time to deal with the situation without the whole world knowing, which they certainly would have, had we had to recapitalise. We responded as well as we could and then – looked at our shoes.

Peter Kuhn

Use peer review to minimise risk

The need to put up large financial guarantees in order to secure certain rights was an issue that IMG had to face with increasing frequency as time went on. We would represent a rights holder for an agreed commission, and in return guarantee that they would receive a certain minimum amount of money. That was not a problem if we got our figures right, but could be risky if not.

On one memorable occasion, my father read in the newspaper that one of our senior soccer executives had guaranteed FIFA $1bn for their rights – and this was the first time he had heard about it. It is one thing to bet the company, but it is quite another to do so without asking the owner of the company first!

In the event, it turned out that the bid had not been made with any intention of succeeding. It was done to highlight a perceived rigged system by an executive who knew that there would be plenty of time to get formal approvals in the unlikely event that FIFA started to negotiate with us in good faith.

However, the incident helped illustrate the need to manage and control large risks. The need for systems and checks becomes more acute when the interests of the company and the employee are not always perfectly aligned. If IMG made a large guarantee and all went well, then the executive responsible would, not unreasonably, expect to receive a large bonus. However, if anything went wrong and if IMG ended up losing lots of money, many people might suffer through reduced bonuses while the executive concerned would, most likely, still receive their salary. In the worst-case scenario, the whole company could be wiped out. The risks are not symmetrical. As the company grew, and more executives were offering guarantees, it became clear that systems had to be put in place to counter this problem.

The solution was the establishment of a Senior Executive Committee that had to sign off on any guarantees. This ensured that there was a consensus among senior executives – rather than it falling to one person – before a big bet was placed, and it gave our most experienced executives a chance to ask the tough questions and remedy any obvious flaws in the proposed plan before it was too late. Recommendations were rarely turned down, mainly because it was understood that the ideas proposed had the broad support of the most senior executives before they were proposed. But the system made everyone stop and think that little bit harder before taking the risk. With greater account-ability to your peers comes greater care.

Breck McCormack

Adopt policy by consensus

For a time at IMG, I sat on the Administrative Operations Committee. We met to determine cost-cutting measures to reduce overhead in the company, primarily travel expenses. With executives travelling all over the world, so much money was spent on airfares and hotels that we were looking at ways to bring down the costs. In my first meeting, the discussion was around airfares and company air miles. Mark said to me: 'Gary, what do you think of the company using the air miles that people earn?' His suggestion was that if I, as an individual, had earned 50,000 miles worth of free travel as a result of the number of flights I had taken, what about the company claiming them and using them for business purposes? I said that I didn't think that it was a very good idea. Why, he countered. I said that it was not great because there was no such thing as a corporate account. People had individual accounts on which they earned free miles, and you would be taking away a perk, which would be bad for morale. The loss of morale and goodwill wouldn't be worth the gain of the cost benefits for the company.

In typical Mark fashion, instead of leaving it there, he asked me what my solution would be. I suggested that if a company executive had enough air miles for, say, a business-class ticket costing $7,000, and the executive was authorised to fly business class, the company should allow the employee to use those miles for the ticket. The company would then pay the executive 50 per cent, so $3,500. The executive would receive a lump sum in cash, and the company would save $3,500, so everyone would be happy. Mark agreed it was a good idea and it became a policy that lasted for years. The point was that what was effectively a cost-saving measure had been produced in a consensual environment. The idea had come from the staff committee, making people happier to adopt it rather than it sounding like an edict from the top.

Gary Swain

Cash is king

Christopher Lewinton was a successful businessman who served on IMG's advisory board for many years. One message that he constantly stressed was the importance of cash flow. He would continually remind us that most businesses fail due to cash flow problems, even if they had a good concept and might otherwise be viable.

My father was also acutely aware of the importance of positive cash flow. He stressed to all executives the importance of doing barter deals that would help us reduce our cash outlays. I tried to stay extremely focused on the importance of cash flow as we expanded our business in Asia. We had one office in Hong Kong when I arrived in 1990, and we ended up with 14 offices across the region by the time I left in 2005. But each time we opened a new office, we tried to make sure that we could do so in a cash-positive way.

Normally, this meant that we needed to have a flagship project or event that was going to be profitable before we established a presence on the ground. We would start by travelling to a new market on a regular basis in order to get to know the key players before we even thought about setting up a local presence. In an ideal world, we would sell title sponsorship to an event in the new market before we set up a local office. We would price the title sponsorship at a level that would make it profitable even after taking into account the people that we would need to put on the ground. We would then be able to hire a local person knowing that the cost of doing so had already been covered by the original event budget.

If we hired the right person, they would then be able to generate additional profits by selling secondary sponsorships to the original event. But they would be able to work on new projects as well since the original event would not occupy 100 per cent of their time for the full year. In this way, the person running the local office would have a good flagship event that would allow them to meet with all of the potential sponsors in the market to discuss sponsorship of the original event. But while they were meeting everyone, they could also learn what else the potential local sponsors might like to do. If we could create a new event for them based on this knowledge, then we could continue to expand our portfolio of events in the new market in a cash-positive way.

Breck McCormack

Know your numbers

The concept of fiscal management and responsibility has been with me since I started studying at the Mark H. McCormack Department of Sport Management. I remember the impression that Mark would willingly spend money in certain areas when he believed it to be correct, but would call out someone who overspent on an expense account. I picked up on the fact that fiscal responsibility is required whatever your role, and for you to really understand how a company operates, you need to be involved in budget management.

It constantly surprises me how many people are happy to spend money but are unwilling to own or manage budgets. I quickly discovered that budget management allowed me to understand how a company was making money, and what the impact of any ideas that I presented to executives was likely to be. If I didn't understand where the priorities of the company were, and consequently where funds were being directed, I was not going to get far. I try to explain that to account executives who say they don't want to get involved. I say you are shooting yourself in the foot. Understanding the budget is a vital skill.

Zaileen Janmohamed

9

The entrepreneurial spirit

*This may still be one of the better ways to start a
business: what are you really passionate about in
life and is there any way to make a living at it?*

MHM believed that starting a business was as much an emotional
as a financial or professional commitment. His entrepreneurial
spirit was founded in his love of golf and in the idea that he had
to make a business and a career out of it, which, as we've seen,
led to the growth and development of IMG as a sports industry
powerhouse. But he was equally clear that starting a business
is no time for getting caught up in the romance of it all. Being
entrepreneurial is often a balancing act between seemingly
contrary instincts and ideas. Chapter 9 offers some stories and
examples to help you find your way through.

For sports entrepreneur Feng Tao, MHM's thinking opened
his eyes to the possibilities of combining sport and business,
just as the market was opening up in his native China. Among
all the things he learned from *What They Don't Teach You ...*,
he identifies the wisdom of thinking long term and signing
long-term contracts as the key lesson, a seemingly counter-
intuitive approach in a market where billionaires can be made
(and destroyed) in a matter of just a few years. Feng Tao,
though, sees the value in longer-term relationship building to
support his growth. Veteran business leader Sir Christopher
Lewinton supports the wisdom of taking the long view. The

lesson is clear: **look ahead, even at the expense of short-term gain**.

One of MHM's original smarts was to 'know when you're lucky'. For IMG's Peter German, luck is when skill and opportunity come together: 'You create your own luck by seeing the opportunity and being in the position to seize it.' This was certainly the case when a BBC cameramen's strike forced the IMG Media team into televising golf – and ultimately led to the creation of European Tour Productions, now one of the biggest producers and distributors of golf programming in the world. **Don't underestimate the opportunities afforded by timing and happenstance** – and position yourself well to take advantage of the opportunities that may come your way. Having the right information to hand can give you first mover advantage when the time comes. Sebastian Coe witnessed first-hand how effectively MHM garnered what he needed to put him on the front foot.

MHM's lessons around thinking small and retaining an entrepreneurial spirit struck a chord with Peter McKelvey, who tries to put this thinking into practice in his own company. As you grow, **keep a balance between systems/bureaucracy and flexibility**. You might need it. MHM felt that companies tended to be 'inherently conservative'. Guard against that and **don't be afraid of experimentation and risk**. Find the risk appetite that works for you and hold your nerve if not everything goes to plan. For Bob Kain, risk-taking is just another form of R&D: 'If you are not taking any risks, you are not moving forwards.' **Always look for opportunities to improve the markets you work in**, something practised in spades by IMG and MHM in the world of sports, as former European Tour boss Ken Schofield recalls. This might also be a case of going global, taking advantage of international expansion to complement local success.

Business success can lead to **complacency**, which **must be fought against at all costs**. Keep a close eye on your competition and challenge received wisdom, both within and beyond your organisation. Hold on to a can-do attitude and don't be afraid to change your mind as you grow and develop. When Ian Todd joined Nike, association with the stuffy, blazer-wearing types at the IOC seemed inconceivable, but their successful sponsorship of the Sydney 2000 Olympics changed hearts and minds. John Skipper reminds us of the importance of trusting your instinct, but **beware ego at all costs**. Casey Wasserman passes on his grandfather's mantra that you 'need to park your ego at the door every morning'. Business success comes from the quality of the products and services you offer and the company you keep rather than individual capability, no matter how impressive that might be.

MHM ended *What They Don't Teach You ...* by identifying three characteristics of champions – whether in sport or business. First, they don't dwell on their accomplishments, always being ambitious for the next challenge. Second, they can reach peak performance when they need to. Third, in a champion's mind, he is never ahead and has to keep striving. Not a bad way to think about an entrepreneurial spirit from which we can all learn.

The long-term entrepreneur

I bought *What They Don't Teach You at Harvard Business School* at a bookstore in Beijing in the late 1990s. At that time there was no sports marketing industry in China. We had zero knowledge on the subject, and the book really opened my eyes. I saw for the first time that I could combine business and sport, and it encouraged me to set up my own company.

Sport in China has traditionally been run by the government, and while other industries have embraced globalisation, the sports industry lagged behind. In 2014, that changed when the government issued a new policy, stating that by 2025, the value of the sports industry should be raised to around $800bn. It introduced tax breaks and relaxed administrative barriers to encourage private and foreign capital investment. Immediately, sport became a hot topic in China. It is why Chinese conglomerate Wanda Group acquired Swiss-based Infront Sports and Media, which distributes broadcasting rights for some of the world's biggest sporting events. And why internet giant Ali Baba moved into sport. But it became apparent that, while there was plenty of money in the industry, there was not enough knowledge. Several thousand start-ups received investment, but 80 to 90 per cent of them were finished after twenty months, as they had misunderstood the nature of the business.

The key element I took from the Harvard book was the importance of signing long-term contracts with players, rights holders or broadcasters, which allows you to develop your business plan and build up a business. But in China, no one thinks that long term. The sports industry is about people and relationships, which makes it very different to the fast-growth businesses in China where you can become a billionaire in two to three years. I am trying to educate people to be patient, to think long term, and to agree – and importantly stick to what has been agreed – in a long-term contract.

I say to a lot of my friends that they have to read *What They Don't Teach You …* I make all my new staff read it, as I see it as the entry point for the industry. However, it is not just for the sports industry, but for business in general. We learned how to do negotiations, and how to present ourselves, and the company. The book is in my blood. We were one of the pioneers of the industry in China and remain one of the leading players. And that is in large part because of the lessons that we learned from Mark's book, primarily our understanding that in a people-based business, it is all about long-term relationships.

Feng Tao

Play the long game

I was running the shaving company Wilkinson Sword at a time when we were hot property but had very little money. Gillette was the dominant figure in the market, but we were making inroads, and I wanted to capitalise on our momentum. I had a thought as to how to increase visibility within the confines of a small marketing budget. My idea was to persuade the golfer, Arnold Palmer, who was the biggest name imaginable at the time, to say that he shaved with Wilkinson. I approached Mark, having never met him, and suggested my idea. Mark said that in principle the idea was fine, but that Arnold would not do a deal with a sponsor he hadn't met, and we would therefore need a meeting together. As a big golf fan, I thought, 'this gets better and better'. I met Arnold and Mark for breakfast, and all went well. We shook hands, and letters of agreement followed, in which we agreed to pay a $30k retainer. About a month or two went by before I got a call from the parent company to say that I had to cancel the deal as the budget just wasn't there. I was mortified. My protestations fell on deaf ears, however, and I was simply told that I had to get out of it.

The call I then made to Mark was one of the most difficult things I have had to do. I was full of trepidation as I started explaining what had happened and how my parent company had told me that I could not go through with my commitment. There was a brief pause before Mark said, 'OK, no problem, don't worry about it. But let's stay in touch.'

I was enormously grateful. His generous action had got me out of a very difficult and embarrassing situation, and I told him how much I appreciated it. True to his word, he stayed in touch. His graciousness turned into a strong personal friendship and business relationship leading to countless commercial transactions.

He had made a judgement, correctly, that his gesture at that time would lead to many, many benefits over the long term. From

Mark I saw the wisdom of making careful judgements of people, and coupled with trust and confidence, building long-term relationships. I have spent my life running global businesses and know that if you make the right judgement, and trust someone, it will reap dividends. I once heard it said that if you throw your bread on troubled waters it comes back as smoked salmon sandwiches. But you have to make the right judgement, and that comes with experience. When you have made a few mistakes, and have had your fingers burned, you develop a sense of whom you can trust. That will then guide your judgement.

Sir Christopher Lewinton

Create your own luck

In the 1970s and early 1980s, outside broadcasting was very limited, and as a consequence there was little golf coverage on TV. In countries like Germany and France, golf was a niche sport and even in Spain they had little interest and even less understanding. When Seve Ballesteros, the Spanish golfer, was at the height of his fame I remember a Spanish broadcaster wanting to broadcast live for twenty minutes on the last day of a tournament and being perplexed as to why we could not guarantee that Seve would be standing on the tee at the exact moment they came on air.

In the UK, the BBC were the host broadcasters for several events, including the prestigious World Match Play Championship, owned and staged by IMG, while TWI, our television production and distribution subsidiary, was involved with production and distribution around the world. One year, they were due to cover the World Match Play in the UK, but the BBC cameramen went on strike just days before the event was due to start. We had sold TV rights all around the world to those countries interested in golf – mainly Commonwealth countries, Japan and US, and we had a contract with the title sponsor that we needed to satisfy. As far as we were concerned, we had to deliver. Rather than cancelling or postponing the event we brought in our own cameras, cameramen and directors from TWI. While they had the technical expertise and personnel, they had never before covered a golf event live, and it was quite a hairy experience. We were in uncharted water with little time to prepare. In the end, all went well. The pictures weren't shown in the UK but went where they were supposed to go around the world.

Not long after that I was in a meeting with Mark and a couple of other senior IMG executives in a hotel in London. Mark announced that we were now going to televise every European Tour golf event. Our initial reaction was that he was out of his mind. It was not just the logistics, but how on earth would we fund it? Mark elaborated, saying that we should set up a joint venture with the PGA European Tour, the organisation that operates the leading men's professional golf tours in Europe. He had realised that with every single event televised sponsorship would grow exponentially.

It proved to be prescient. Sky was in its embryonic stage and we were able to capitalise on their entry to the broadcasting market. The joint venture that we set up with the European Tour runs to this day, under the title European Tour Productions. It is the world's most prolific producer and distributor of golf programming with an annual output of over 700 hours.

The BBC strike had given Mark the opportunity to demonstrate IMG's capability to televise golf events. It may not have felt lucky at the time, with everyone in a panic to deliver television coverage in a way that we had never done before. I doubt that Mark intellectualised it that week. His first thought would have been to avoid lost revenue from non-delivery of television coverage. But once the dust had settled, he could see that the strike was actually a stroke of luck, and that armed with this display of capability, he could convince the European Tour that the joint venture was the way forward. I've heard it said that luck is when skill and opportunity come together. You create your own luck by seeing the opportunity and being in the position to seize it.

Peter German

Keep it simple

In the early 1980s, golf coverage on television was pretty dire. The only people involved were major terrestrial broadcasters and we were at their mercy. We had a lot of challenges in different countries where the local networks were trying to provide coverage but it is very difficult to do well with limited experience and no dedicated personnel. Unless you are used to televising golf, you may not be aware of where to put the cameras in order to cover the movement of the ball in the air, for example.

At that point, TWI, the sister company to IMG [now IMG Media], had good experience of televising events in other sports, but hadn't covered golf tournaments. Mark came to us suggesting that we take control of the production and broadcasting of golf tournaments so that we could then sell the pictures to different TV stations. We agreed to come together to develop a non-network television idea, and then decided to produce the actual pictures for every tournament starting from scratch. We understood golf, we could use dedicated staff, TWI had the television capability, we would be able to increase sponsorship … the reasons for doing so were overwhelming. It was so blindingly obvious, but someone had to see it in the first place. Sometimes you don't have to look far to find the inspiration. Now European Tour Productions, the joint venture set up between IMG and the PGA European Tour, is the biggest producer and distributor of golf programming in the world.

George O'Grady

Embrace a can-do culture

Mark loved entrepreneurialism and positively encouraged it. You would never be out of order if you came up with a madcap scheme for something. Very often someone would come to us and say, 'can we do this?' And we would say, well, we didn't think so, but why not? Almost everything is possible. Say 'yes' and then think about 'how' is very much the IMG way of thinking.

Take the 1990 Stockholm World Equestrian Games. That was the biggest tented event that I ran. We needed 20,000 square metres of marquees just for the horses. It was quite an operation that got bigger and bigger as the event drew closer.

When it came to hospitality, there were two choices. One was to build a hospitality village for all the sponsors out in Djurgarden, a park that was quite a long way from the Olympic stadium, where most things happened. Or we could close down Valhallavägen, the equivalent of London's Oxford Street, at midnight one night, build hospitality units for 750 people from 20 to 30 different companies and map it all out by morning, and then put a red carpet from the units across the pavement into the stadium for the guests to walk on. That was the route we took. We got the police to approve it, and we built it all in six hours. By 6 a.m. that morning, we were virtually ready. By 8 a.m. the food had arrived and we were all systems go. The clients wouldn't even have known that they were walking on a main thoroughfare. What we achieved was incredible, but it was all down to good workmen, good people and good suppliers and the 'can-do' attitude that came from the very top at IMG.

Jeremy Palmer-Tomkinson

Plan ahead

As I was approaching the end of my tennis career, I was trying to figure out what I could do next. It was quite daunting to be only in your mid to late twenties and already to be thinking, 'what else can I do?'

Mark gave me a lot of good advice. He suggested a number of things like going back to school, being a teaching pro or a touring pro. He also said to try television and commentating. I was hesitant, saying that I was quite shy and didn't think I'd be able to do it. But he argued that I loved tennis and I loved watching it. His best advice was that I try doing television work while I was still playing. He urged me to start planning before the last day came. So for around six months before I retired, that's exactly what I did. I would come into the studio and just commentate on perhaps a set at the US Open or Indian Wells. That way, I could see if I liked it and if the television people liked me. Because I was still playing, I just saw it as a secondary thing, something I was trying out, which took the pressure off. People also still looked at me as a tennis player. The attitude was: 'Oh, here's Mary Joe. She's just played her match and now she's going to do a bit of commentating.' It was a soft start, and perfect for me.

Television turned out to be a good move, and now I've been commentating for seventeen years. I owe that career change to Mark and to his vision of getting ahead of the ball and thinking of things before decision day comes. It's a lesson I've always remembered.

Mary Joe Fernandez

Don't accept industry norms

When IMG became a serious player in the modelling world, it turned our industry on its head. They came in with a business-like, professional approach and set the marker, which others followed. So much of the industry is better for the stability and professionalism that IMG provided.

When setting up IMG Models, IMG took a hard look at the industry through their own business lens and rejected practices that had become the industry norm. One example was mother agency commission rate. If you discovered a model in a remote location like Peru, and saw that he or she had the potential to work internationally, you would make an arrangement with the model's local agency whereby that agency received a standard percentage of the model's commission, for the duration of their modelling career. IMG came into the game and saw that the situation was inequitable. If you had a model who was so successful that the commission rate was for any reason reduced, you could be locked into an agreement paying more to someone in Peru than you earn yourself. IMG soon started stipulating that, if for any reason, we should have to offer a model a commission reduction along the line, we would ask for the mother agency rate to be reduced proportionately. That was just good business sense, but it was revolutionary for the industry.

Professional standards were raised too. Magazines would book a shoot for a model in Tahiti, and have flights, models and photographers organised without anyone having checked whether there was a need for a licence to shoot or conduct business there. IMG said that our models would not work anywhere on the planet without a visa and the rest of the industry followed suit. It was the way that IMG operated in every sector and modelling would be no different.

This reputation for professionalism helped with our recruitment. We follow girls from age thirteen, and more often than not, you'll be dealing with parents when girls are first signed. When you talk to a parent about the players and events that IMG look after in the sporting sector, they start to become much more comfortable. If you can manage the careers of the Williams sisters or Rafael Nadal, or Tiger Woods, then you can manage the career of their child and apply the same professionalism. As outsiders, IMG's adherence to their own principled and ethical approach, rather than adapting to the modelling industry norm, proved to be a huge selling point.

Jeni Rose

Master first mover advantage

In athletics, the use of the word 'amateur' withered on the vine. There was no traumatic parting of the ways as there had been in other sports. We transitioned into a system where if you were good enough, you got invited to the top athletics meetings, and sponsors came knocking.

In 1979, I unexpectedly broke three world records. That took me from being someone known in the sport to someone on the front page of newspapers. My father was clear that while he would coach me, I should establish a relationship with an organisation that would be able to handle any commercial pressures. I spoke to a number of people from different sports, as this was an untrodden path in athletics. When I joined IMG, we were both trying to find our way in the new athletic world. It was absolutely a partnership, to the extent that my first main contact at IMG remains a very close friend and someone whose advice I still seek.

When I first met Mark, I was advised that the meeting was really just an introduction and would only last five or six minutes, given the constraints on his diary. In fact, we sat talking for the best part of an hour. There was no small talk as you might have expected. Instead, we discussed what was going to happen in athletics. The big challenge was the word 'professional'. While it hadn't really come into the lexicon of athletics, it was a word without definition in the Eastern bloc or former Soviet Union. The biggest challenge was preventing the sport from breaking in two. The risk was that we would end up with two very different sports on different circuits, and athletes like me would never race against Eastern Europeans. Mark was interested in the landscape and the way I saw it. I was young but I could see the practical challenges and I also had an understanding of the history. He picked my brains as to where I thought athletics was heading. He was a very, very good listener. His questions were penetrative, and he was able to sift the wheat from the chaff and refine his thinking around the subject.

I have no doubt that he asked me those very detailed questions in order to work out how he was going to make a mark, and become a market leader in the sport. I'm sure he was asking exactly the same questions of a group of golfers in the clubhouse at Muirfield or wherever, twenty years earlier, with similar results. The only sustainable competitive advantage we have in life is absorbing information quicker and turning it around faster than the next person. Mark was a master at that.

Sebastian Coe

Go with your gut

I realised just the other day that I did something like Mark. I was giving an interview and I was asked a complicated question about how we kept up with consumer trends and changing viewing habits. I answered by going into some detail about research capabilities, focus groups, reading material and that sort of thing. And then I laughed and said, 'When all is said and done, after that, I consult my gut. I go with my instinct and make a decision.' That was core to Mark's way of thinking. Throughout your career you have different experiences that help towards an instinctual decision-making process. If I had to choose between fabulous research and making an instinctive decision based on previous experience and common sense, I would choose the latter in almost every situation.

That is perhaps the difference between what they do and don't teach you at Harvard. My job prior to my current role was as head of content for ESPN. Making creative content decisions is particularly about instinct and gut as opposed to analysis. You could articulate the difference between the two by noting that they only teach you case histories and methodologies for analytics and situational metrics at Harvard. They don't teach you the other because they can't teach you the other. But in many cases, like creative decision-making, it is equally if not more valid.

John Skipper

It's not about you, but the company

My grandfather [Hollywood studio head (MCA) and talent agent] Lew Wasserman, was a great friend and mentor of Mark's. They spent a lot of time together and Mark has written about some of the advice that Lew passed on to him. One lesson concerned ego. Mark describes it as a double-edged sword – the gasoline that drives us to work harder, but at the same time capable of distorting judgement, which is why it must be managed. He wrote that Lew once told him: 'The only way service businesses like ours can work is if you park your ego at the door every morning.'

Lew's advice was, he said: 'Don't sell yourself – sell the company.'

It was certainly advice that Mark took to heart. Mark was all about IMG rather than himself, and would never talk about his successes, rather the company's. I was the beneficiary of similar advice myself: 'Don't stand under the light too long, it will fade your suit.' I have similarly tried to take it to heart. Our success is defined by the talent we represent and their success, not our ability to promote ourselves. The same rule applies, pretty much regardless of industry. A manufacturer will be judged by the quality and success of its product, not the ability of the CEO to grab headlines.

Casey Wasserman

Once an athlete …

Mark was an athlete at the start of his career, and once an athlete certain traits stay with you. People talked about 'Mark the Shark' when he was negotiating, and a little part of me relates to that. I was very aggressive and competitive on the court and he was competitive in his line of work. He wanted to be number one and to stay there.

He was also very competitive on the tennis court. When you played with Mark you had to win. I always told him that I preferred to play *against* him because it was too much pressure to be *with* him. I said that I would rather play at any Grand Slam than play doubles with him, and any time I could get out of it I did. But it was part of his personality, and with anything related to sport or business, he just couldn't switch off.

One of the things Mark always used to say to me is: what is the next stage? You can never rest on your laurels or allow yourself to get complacent, because you are only ever as good as your last match. There is always someone, somewhere in the world, training to beat you. He was so right with that philosophy, and he applied it in the same way to IMG. To stay at the top you always need to look ahead.

I also admired his ability to juggle all his travel commitments and his ability to function in so many different time zones. That is not easy. To be upbeat and on the phone at 4.30 a.m., and have the discipline to do that day in, day out is very impressive. He clearly wasn't driven by money, and was passionate about what he was doing. It is another trait that you see in successful professional sportspeople.

Monica Seles

Don't be afraid to change your mind

At its outset, IMG was very anti-establishment. It was effectively creating a new industry and had little time for the 'old guard'. But Mark soon worked out that establishments such as the R&A and Wimbledon would be around forever whereas individual clients would not. He saw the value in cultivating those relationships and was quick to change his mind.

When I left IMG I went to work for Nike in their sports marketing division. They were similarly anti-establishment, wanting to project an 'edgy' image. But taking my lead from

Mark, I could see that you would limit yourself to a certain size by taking that approach. Just months before the Sydney 2000 Olympics, I got a call from the International Olympic Committee (IOC) saying that Reebok, who were meant to be sponsoring the Australian team, would no longer be doing so and would Nike like to do it? There were roughly six months to go and thousands of bits of specialised apparel to be designed, manufactured and delivered, which was a logistical challenge in itself. However, my biggest challenge was in getting Nike to agree.

When I first broached the subject the answer was a flat no. There was not a chance that a company like Nike wanted to be associated with the Olympics and a body like the IOC, stuffed full of blazer-wearing types. That was not Nike's image. I persisted, urging them to think beyond the personalities to what it is that the IOC controls. The Olympics is the biggest sporting event in the world. It was being held in Australia, boosting the host nation's chances of winning more gold medals than ever before, and we had the chance to equip that team. Much against the will of a lot of people at Nike, we took up the contract and it proved to be a huge success. The company subsequently reversed its antipathy to all things establishment, and is now successfully involved with a vast number of teams, clubs and federations. Being at IMG had taught me that a company can – and should – change its mind as it grows and develops.

Ian Todd

The company you keep

As the newly appointed managing director of IMG Canada, I thought I had the world by the tail. The Canadian office, long treated as a satellite offshoot of the US business, was on a bit of a roll. We were expanding our golf business, increasing our influence in tennis and taking the world by storm in figure skating. However, as I presented my five-year growth plan to senior management,

Mark asked: 'How can we possibly become the dominant agency in Canada without representing hockey stars?'

I explained that the relationship between hockey players and agents was rooted in local connections, built over decades, and then indicated that it was a 'private club' of insiders and it would take years to develop the relationships necessary to break into the club. His response was to ask who the biggest star was at the time. Without doubt that was Wayne Gretzky, represented by the agency CorpSport.

Within the year, CorpSport had merged its operations with IMG Canada – with the new IMG Hockey under the direction of Wayne's trusted agent, Mike Barnett. And IMG's influence in hockey went from zero to unparalleled virtually overnight. That was vintage Mark McCormack. He never saw challenges as insurmountable – merely obstacles to be overcome with creative thinking.

That lesson returned to my mind several years later in Charlotte, North Carolina. Mark agreed to allow me to open a new office in the southeastern US, as I was convinced that there were opportunities to be had. It was a growing banking centre and the undisputed home of one of the hottest sports in America – NASCAR.

We set about trying to convince the biggest star of the NASCAR Sprint Cup Series, Jeff Gordon, to join IMG's stable of champions. We reasoned that representing Jeff would give IMG instant credibility in racing circles and put us onto the path of growing the new office into a profitable operation.

We did. He did. And the Charlotte office took off. Mark's idea to align ourselves with the most influential athletes in every sport proved to be a cornerstone of IMG's success, from Arnold Palmer to Killy, Pele, Agassi, Gretzky, Tiger, and dozens more to follow. Lesson learned. The greater the influence of the people with whom you are connected, the greater your influence over the market in which you operate.

Michael Wright

When direct control matters

My father always understood the value of television. Not only was TWI (now IMG Media) the most profitable division in the company, it was also the engine that made it possible for us to earn more money from the events we ran and the clients that we represented.

Up until 1987, we used an agent to distribute the television programming that we owned and represented in Asia outside of Japan. In those days, the rights fees we could generate were simply too small to justify the expense of distributing the programming ourselves. However, things changed with the advent of new private television stations and cable companies in competition with the various government-owned stations.

My father understood how important it was to have our finger on the pulse of the Asian television market. Our relationships with clients such as Wimbledon or sponsors like Alfred Dunhill were based on maximum global coverage and exposure. We might need to secure live network coverage at the expense of the short-term benefits of doing a more lucrative deal with a cable company with limited viewership. That might not tie in with an agent's interests.

It was also important for us to develop direct relationships with the TV stations, as evidenced in our role in creating the Chinese National Football League.

The China Football Association (CFA) was desperate to improve the quality of football in China after repeated failures to qualify for the World Cup. It was felt that the only way to improve the standard of play was to create a league. However, the CFA considered this too expensive an option.

Our good relationship with China's national broadcaster, CCTV, provided a solution. CCTV confirmed that, if a football league was created, they would commit to showing at least one game a week live on national TV. We went to potential sponsors and got their commitment to support the league so long as we could promise them live weekly television exposure on CCTV. With sponsorship commitments in hand, we went back to the CFA and guaranteed them the money that they needed to set up and run the league. The CFA, CCTV and our sponsors were happy, and the league became one of IMG's most profitable events for many years to come. On the back of that success, we asked CCTV if there was any other sport that they could commit to broadcasting in the same time slot once the football season was over. Yes, they replied, basketball. Since there was not yet a basketball league in China, we went to the Chinese Basketball Association and went through the same process all over again. Armed with guaranteed television exposure on CCTV, we were able to launch the first-ever basketball league in China on a profitable basis.

Knowing what television exposure could be achieved was vital to the success of virtually every event that we created or represented. And once it became business critical, it was not something to be left in the hands of agents. We needed direct control to negotiate the deals and form the relationships that allowed us to take advantage of the opportunities available to us.

Breck McCormack

Don't be afraid of risk

When Mark first started out, he was operating as an agent, which involved little if any risk and low capital. IMG could have stayed that way, but we decided we wanted to move into owning assets and operating events. That was absolutely the right decision, but it was an interesting transition.

In my domain, which was tennis, we knew about sponsorship and television, we represented the stars, and I thought it was time to start owning events. After doing well in Italy and Germany, I saw an opportunity to buy an event in the US. A guy called Butch Buchholz wanted to start a tournament in Miami, and we were happy for him to front it and run it while we underwrote it. We didn't want to be front and centre as there was a view that we were too controlling already. However, while it proved to be a good idea in the long run, at the time we were a little too early – we had gone too far, too fast. We ended up losing $1m, which was a significant sum for us at that time.

When I had to tell Mark, there was a group of us sitting around the table, and I knew that the others were thinking, 'there goes my bonus this year', and they were angry. I felt terrible for them. Mark, however, was great. He defended me to the other guys, saying that it was the right thought process, and that we should be owning assets. He pumped me up, and was clearly worried that I might never take another risk, which he didn't want. His approach was, keep going, you are on the right track and this was just a hiccup. It was a hairy moment, but his support for me was brilliant.

Fast-forward two or three years, and I was negotiating with the Association of Tennis Professionals (ATP) over the newly established ATP tour. We went to Hamilton Jordan [then chief executive of the ATP] and said that we wanted to run the ATP finals in Frankfurt, sell title sponsorship to the tour, and sell the television rights globally to ATP tournaments. Jordan said: 'I'm never going to give you all three of those things or I might just as well have IMG stamped on my forehead.' He really wanted to split the three up and not have one agency in charge of everything. But we held firm. We said we were prepared to pay $34m over three years, 1990 to 1992, but that we had to have all three elements. It was a brand-new tour for the ATP and they needed some capital to get it off the ground. Jordan saw that, and said, 'OK, for that money, I'll have the stamp.'

It was a good negotiation for us, and in the end we generated $100m over three years for the ATP. If Mark had not supported me so wholeheartedly over the Miami deal, it would have been a lot harder to find an appetite for even greater risks. We got good at taking risks and figuring out what we could and couldn't do.

Not all would make money, but if you are not taking any risks, you are not moving forwards. In a way, taking risks to explore new opportunities is just another form of R&D.

Bob Kain

Think small to grow bigger

The classic dilemma of a growing company is how to retain an entrepreneurial culture and be open to new ideas. Although I never did business with Mark, and only met him socially, I read *What They Don't Teach You at Harvard Business School* over twenty years ago, and parts of it have stuck with me throughout my career. One philosophy I took on board was overcoming the difficulty of maintaining the ésprit de corps of an entrepreneurial organisation as you grow in size.

When you are a small company, you are nimble and there is a sense of immediacy and excitement as you strive to grow. But then when you do grow, you become more bureaucratic and it becomes harder and harder to retain that small company culture.

When I joined L.E.K. Consulting over 25 years ago we were about 10 per cent of our current size. As we grew, I remembered Mark's comments about ésprit de corps. Now, as president of the Americas, I do many things to try to maintain that entrepreneurial culture. I try to have small working groups, a technique they also apply in the marines, and one that helps people feel that they have ownership of something. It doesn't matter if it's client-facing or an internal function like human resources. When an organisation or the units within it get too large, diseconomies of scale creep in, normally through poor communication, lack of motivation, or lack of ownership.

We have a very flat structure that is not hierarchical, which makes it easier for all voices to be heard at all levels. People want to see from the top that there is a culture of change, and a willingness to listen to new ideas, rather than chastising someone for asking stupid questions or asking to change things. We don't put titles on business cards, which helps create a sense of equality. Apart from a logo and address change, my business card now is the same as it was 25 years ago. We also create frequent opportunities to socialise, to break down the big company barrier. But it is a constant battle that you need to keep fighting, and something that I work hard at every day and try to make sure feeds through the organisation. It is even in our recruiting mantra. We say that we have the culture of a small firm with the benefits of a large multinational. With our new recruits who start every year, I always say: I want you to refer to L.E.K. in the first person. I never want to hear a question like, 'Why don't they open an office in Atlanta?' I want to hear, 'Why don't we?' It's important for maintaining camaraderie and a sense of togetherness. Sometimes you need to think small in order to keep growing.

Peter McKelvey

Improving the marketplace

The official world golf rankings is now over 30 years old, and continues to grow in significance. Its implementation is due in large part to Mark, and professional golf is better for it.

Mark had been trying to devise a concept by which you could rank the best players in the world. Golfers had previously been ranked according to the PGA Tour money list, which essentially meant earnings from the US Tour. However, with the rise of more international players, Mark wanted a more representative system. He was introduced to Tony Greer, a civil engineer whose passion was collating statistics, and who had been working on the mechanics of a system for several years. While Tony had the system, Mark sold the concept, securing both our backing at the European Tour and that of the R&A, more or less from day one, and sponsorship from Sony.

The creation of the rankings and the way in which they have

been developed set a template for international golfers to have the opportunity to play in all four majors, three of which are in the US. Had Mark not got the concept established, countless numbers of international players, many of them European, may not have had the opportunity to play the majors, because the criteria might have remained solely the US PGA Tour's own money list. That could well have meant having to play more or less full time in the US in order to qualify. Although many golfers now do play in the US, the great majority still play internationally and support their home tours. The establishment of the world rankings made that possible. And there's no doubt that it was Mark's understanding, his drive, and his presence that got the rankings accepted.

People might not always have been in favour of the direction I was taking the Tour, or our close relationship with IMG, but I think all of them would have seen that the rankings was a natural fit. As to our relationship generally, there were two responses. The first was that while IMG was our biggest partner, there was no exclusivity and anyone else who could have helped in the same way was welcome to do so. That led to the second point – there was no one else who was being anything like as supportive in trying to grow the European Tour for the good of the game. The rankings were an extension of those efforts. They are a great example of how improving the marketplace can be a good thing for everyone involved.

Ken Schofield

Go global

For the NFL to continue to grow, we have to find a way to develop a fan base internationally. That means educating people outside the United States about the rules of the game and helping them to develop a passion for it. Given the complexity of the rules, American football takes longer to understand and a greater commitment to learning than say soccer or basketball, where the game is more intuitive.

Mark had creative ideas as to how we could help garner interest in the NFL overseas. He always maintained that we had to make the 'real' product, as in the regular season games as opposed to exhibitions, available to an international audience. He felt that the idea of bringing the intensity of real league games, where the results mattered, to a foreign audience was critical in order to help people get a true flavour and an understanding of the game.

He also stressed the importance of creating television shows that not only aired highlights for those that know the game, but that also included educational pieces to help make people comfortable and to build their knowledge of the rules and strategies.

Unlike a lot of Americans, Mark wasn't afraid to travel and explore the world and he understood the value of that global presence. He had seen that golf and tennis were global sports, and that the same rules could and should apply to football. He intuitively knew that the passion for American pop culture around the world meant that if someone spent time and energy on it, there was a real opportunity.

At the time Mark made these suggestions, the NFL was not yet completely committed to true overseas expansion and marketing of our league. Today we are doing both of the things that Mark suggested, as we are playing regular season games, not just exhibition games, and we are producing high-quality programming developed for fans outside the US on a country- or culture-specific basis. If we had turned this over to Mark in the early 1990s, I have no doubt that today we would have significantly greater and more passionate fan bases throughout the world. He understood better than anyone that the power of sport and competition translate globally, and through his travels he knew how to market a product country by country. Mark was far ahead of his time in terms of his vision and creativity, but the underlying concepts are just as applicable, if not more so, today.

When domestic markets are well developed, look to expand internationally.

Robert Kraft

Enjoy what you do

You have to enjoy what you do. Mark used to say it to me and it is absolutely true. He believed he was very fortunate to have been a scratch golfer, and to have been able to find a way of staying in that world. He enjoyed golf and saw that golfers needed legal and contract representation and went about setting it up on his own. For Mark it wasn't work, it was play. What he did was an extension of enjoying himself. In the same way, I say that there is no such thing as stress. You are just not enjoying yourself. I think that for Mark, every day, including Saturday and Sunday, was work, except that it wasn't work because it was his life.

That however, takes its toll. Life is a balance between family, career and society, and getting that balance right is very difficult. I'm not sure I've been able to balance it and I don't think he did either. IMG was his baby just like WPP is mine, and you become obsessive, putting too much into them and probably spending too much time on them. It's part of the entrepreneurial nature.

Sir Martin Sorrell

The power to endure

To have a company that has been market leader for more than 50 years is a significant achievement. That is even more so when it is a company centred around people and relationships rather than around, for example, manufacturing. When Mark passed away, a lot of people thought that the captain was no longer at the helm so the ship would sink. But the growth has been there for 55 years. For it to survive and prosper after his death is something magical and significant.

When we speak to people, they very often still refer to Mark when they are talking about IMG. It is probably because of the leadership and business model he created, and because he surrounded himself with colleagues who projected his vision, his principles and his advice. It has inspired a lot of people, me in particular, and continues to do so, even among a generation that did not know him.

It hit me when my daughter recently told me that she was reading *What They Don't Teach You at Harvard Business School*. It was not me but a friend that had recommended it to her. They are on the same international business studies course and she had said, 'when you read that book, you will understand business better.' It is all about common sense. In just the same way that kids discover music from a different generation, and will listen to Pink Floyd or The Rolling Stones, these twenty-year-olds had discovered this book and still saw its relevance.

Michel Masquelier

Acknowledgements

Thirty years after the publication of the original edition of *What They Don't Teach You at Harvard Business School*, the book was re-released in the UK, where once again it reached the No. 1 spot for the best-selling business book. Clearly, a new generation of entrepreneurs welcomed Mark McCormack's evergreen wisdom and street-smart advice just as much as their parents did when the book first appeared. In a world driven by algorithms and data, perhaps it was an affirmation that the foundation of success in business isn't solely rooted in a diploma, but also in practical skills on how to effectively manage the people and experiences one encounters daily. One's EQ is surely as vital as one's IQ.

The idea for this book was an answer to one simple question: how could we best pay tribute to this enduring legacy of our father as an author?

One of our dad's favourite adages, which appears in the first Harvard book, was to 'always hire people who are smarter than you'. He certainly practised what he professed, and many of those smarter executives, who worked by his side to help him invent the modern sports marketing industry and build IMG into the world's dominant sports management company, have generously contributed their own valuable insights to this companion volume.

Beyond those IMG 'insiders', dozens of other contributors who were either clients, customers or friends of IMG have shared their perspectives on how our father influenced their own thinking and approach to business. From superstar athletes, to chief executives of Fortune 100 companies, to CEOs of the worlds' leading sports networks to owners and leaders of some of the most successful sports franchises and federations, to the heads of entertainment empires and multilateral institutions fighting global poverty, their collective talent and achievements far outstrip what our father achieved in his life. Together they provide fresh anecdotes and perspectives to illustrate the underlying principles that grounded all of our father's business writing.

We are also grateful to the newest cadre of McCormack disciples – those who never knew him but were influenced by his work and writing, and took the time to share their insights and stories. Our family partnership with the University of Massachusetts, which has renamed their Department of Sport Management in his honour, has ensured that 'what they can't teach you at business school' will be duly integrated with what they *can* teach you – at least at one business school going forward. We are grateful to them for spearheading a myriad of programmes to ensure that the world of Mark H. McCormack continues to expand. In fact, all proceeds our family receives from the publication of this book will be channelled to the Mark H. McCormack Foundation to support these and other educational efforts.

Finally, to Jo Russell, our patient and unflinching editor; Clare Grist Taylor, our dedicated publisher who championed this project from the start; Sarah Wooldridge, the longest-standing IMG London executive and trusted family confidant; and the teams at Profile Books and WME's Publishing Division who worked with our family: all of you played a critical part in bringing this book to fruition. We couldn't have done it without every one of you. Thank you for your time and talents.

The McCormack family

Contributors

SETH ABRAHAM (pages 38 and 127)

Seth Abraham is the founder of sports marketing firm Starship SA, New York, and the former president of HBO sports.

VAL ACKERMAN (pages 28, 77 and 85)

Val Ackerman is the commissioner of the Big East Conference and was the first president of the Women's National Basketball Association.

DICK ALFORD (pages 96, 150, 192 and 207)

Dick Alford was vice president, India and Japan, IMG.

STACEY ALLASTER (pages 21, 108, 120, 148 and 184)

Stacey Allaster is CEO, Professional Tennis at the United States Tennis Association, having previously served as chairman and CEO of the Women's Tennis Association.

JULIAN BRAND (page 15)

Julian Brand spent 32 years at IMG culminating in his role as senior vice president, managing director of Events and Federations.

LORD COE CH, KBE (pages 167, 181 and 227)

Sebastian Coe is president of the International Association of Athletics Federations (IAAF), executive chairman of CSM Sport and Entertainment and chairman of the Sports Honours Committee. He was chairman of the London Organising Committee for the Olympic Games and Paralympic Games, having previously been chairman of the London 2012 bid company.

JEAN COOKE (pages 49 and 109)

Jean Cooke joined IMG in 1992, ultimately becoming vice president, IMG Licensing, and retail director.

LINDA COOPER (pages 27 and 50)

Linda Cooper is the founder of Linda Cooper & Company and Linda Cooper Weddings. She was formerly a vice president at IMG.

JOHN CURRY (pages 70, 92 and 109)

John Curry was chairman of The All England Lawn Tennis Club, and previously chairman of the Club's merchandising committee. He is the founder of Acal plc and Unitech plc.

PETER DAWSON (pages 81 and 128)

Peter Dawson is president of the International Golf Federation, and the former CEO of the R&A.

DONALD DELL (pages 153, 173 and 202)

Donald Dell is group president, Media, Tennis & Events, Lagardere, and a former US Davis Cup Captain. He was the founder of ProServ Agency, the first global agent in pro tennis.

JAYNE EIBEN (page 151)

After leaving IMG, Jayne Eiben worked as a teacher, writer and columnist, and radio commentator on NPR. Jayne is currently the advancement director at Lawrence School in Cleveland, Ohio.

JAN FELGATE (pages 45 and 184)

Jan Felgate is CEO of the ATP Champions Tour and the head of UK tennis division, IMG.

MARY JOE FERNANDEZ (pages 20 and 224)

Mary Joe Fernandez is a tennis commentator and former professional tennis player, having reached a career high ranking of world number four in both singles and doubles.

GAVIN FORBES (pages 56, 130, 174 and 185)

Gavin Forbes is senior vice president and worldwide managing director of IMG's Tennis Division (Men). He is the US tournament board representative for the ATP Tour.

PETER GERMAN (pages 171 and 221)

Peter German is senior vice president, golf tournament director, IMG.

DAVID GILMOUR (pages 13, 166 and 187)

David Gilmour is a life-long entrepreneur and founder of start-ups including Fiji Water, Barrick Gold, and Wakaya Perfection.

TONY GODSICK (pages 53, 113 and 200)

Tony Godsick was senior vice president at IMG before leaving to set up sports and entertainment management firm TEAM8 with Roger Federer.

BERRY GORDY (page 163)

Berry Gordy is the founder of Motown.

CHRIS GORRINGE (pages 36, 81, 110 and 146)

Chris Gorringe is the former CEO of The All England Lawn Tennis Club, a position he held for 26 years.

PETER GRIFFITHS (pages 124 and 182)

Peter Griffiths is chief operating officer, International Division of the National Football League. Previously, he spent almost 27 years at IMG, starting in the finance team and finishing as director of operations of the Sports and Entertainment division.

BERTRAND GROS (pages 18 and 169)

Bertrand Gros is chairman of the board at Rolex.

GEORGE HAMMOND (page 196)

George Hammond is the former golf World Match Play tournament director and official starter.

CHRISTIE HEFNER (page 106)

Christie Hefner is the chairman of Hatch Beauty and the former chairman and CEO, Playboy Enterprises.

NEIL HOBDAY (pages 83, 96, 111 and 199)

Neil Hobday is CEO of the Guards Polo Club. Previously he spent four years with IMG and was also CEO of Loch Lomond Golf Club.

BUZZ HORNETT (pages 35, 65, 88, 110 and 131)

Buzz Hornett is a former senior international vice president, IMG.

ZAILEEN JANMOHAMED (pages 134 and 214)

Zaileen Janmohamed is senior vice president, client services at GMR marketing. She is an alumna of the Isenberg School of Management, University of Massachusetts, Amherst.

ALASTAIR JOHNSTON (pages 34, 59, 68, 134 and 206)

Alastair Johnston was appointed co-CEO of IMG on Mark McCormack's death. He is now vice chairman of IMG and CEO of Arnold Palmer Enterprises.

BOB KAIN (pages 48, 65, 88, 176 and 234)

Bob Kain was appointed president and co-CEO of IMG on Mark McCormack's death. He is the creator and former chairman of the Greater Cleveland Sports Commission, a former senior adviser to Creative Arts Agency, and an executive committee member, USGA.

HOWARD KATZ (pages 22, 90 and 188)

Howard Katz is senior vice president of the National Football League. He is the former president of ABC Sports and executive vice president of ESPN. He was an IMG employee from 1974 to 1983.

SOL KERZNER (page 91)

Sol Kerzner was the founder, CEO and chairman of Kerzner International Hotels. The company developed and operated destination resorts, including Sun City in South Africa, and Atlantis in the Bahamas and Dubai. The company also developed and manages the One&Only Resorts located in The Maldives, Dubai, Mauritius, Mexico, South Africa and The Bahamas.

JEAN-CLAUDE KILLY (pages 27 and 175)

Jean-Claude Killy was co-chairman of the Organising Committee for the 1992 Olympic Winter Games in Albertville, France. As an alpine ski racer, he was triple Olympic champion, winning all three alpine events at the 1968 Winter Olympics.

JIM KIM (pages 11, 25, 67 and 206)

Jim Kim is president of the World Bank Group. Previously he was president of Dartmouth College, and director of the World Health Organization's HIV/AIDS department. He is a co-founder of Partners in Health.

BILLIE JEAN KING (pages 55 and 93)

Billie Jean King is the first woman athlete to receive the US Presidential Medal of Freedom, for her work on and off the tennis court. She is the founder of the Billie Jean King Leadership Initiative, the Women's Sports Foundation, the Women's Tennis Association, and the co-founder of World Team Tennis.

GUY KINNINGS (pages 24, 112, 133 and 208)

Guy Kinnings has been with IMG for over twenty years and is the global head of golf. He is a member of the Board of European Tour Productions.

ROBERT KRAFT (pages 41 and 238)

Robert Kraft is the chairman and CEO of Kraft Group and owner of the NFL's New England Patriots.

PETER KUHN (page 209)

Peter Kuhn was chief financial officer at IMG, before becoming president and CEO then chief investment officer of Parkland Management Company until his retirement.

JAY LAFAVE (page 3)

Arthur J. Lafave, Jr., has held various senior positions at IMG, including senior group vice president, chief financial officer, and vice chairman. He has also been trustee of The Cleveland Orchestra, Cleveland Institute of Music, and Corporate Council of Cleveland Museum of Art.

BERNHARD LANGER (page 170)

Bernhard Langer is a professional golfer. He is a two-time Masters champion and was the sport's first official number one ranked player. He is the recipient of a PGAs of Europe Lifetime Achievement Award.

BOB LATHAM (pages 32, 97 and 127)

Bob Latham, a partner in the Texas-based law firm Jackson Walker LLP, is a World Rugby Executive Committee member, the former chairman of USA Rugby, a former member of the board of directors of the United States Olympic Committee, and a columnist for *SportsTravel* magazine.

MARK LAZARUS (pages 29 and 79)

Mark Lazarus is chairman of NBC Broadcasting and Sports. Previous positions included president of Media and Marketing for CSE and president of Turner Entertainment Group.

SIR CHRISTOPHER LEWINTON (pages 30 and 220)

Sir Christopher Lewinton is chairman of Camper & Nicholsons Marina Investments Ltd and holds advisory roles with Metalmark and J. F. Lehman, New York private equity. Previously he was chairman/CEO of Wilkinson Sword and chairman/CEO of TI Group. He acted as an advisor to Mark H. McCormack and IMG.

TIMO LUMME (pages 82, 156 and 201)

Timo Lumme is the managing director of IOC Television & Marketing Services, the broadcast rights marketing arm of the International Olympic Committee (IOC). Having started his career at IMG, he joined the IOC from ESPN where he was vice president Europe, Middle East and Africa (EMEA).

COLIN MACLAINE (page 114)

Colin Maclaine was captain of the R&A (Royal and Ancient Golf Club). On Mark McCormack's request he became a business adviser to IMG and one of three trustee advisers.

MICHEL MASQUELIER (pages 28, 57, 203 and 240)

Michel Masquelier is chairman, IMG Media. During a career spanning over 30 years at IMG, he has progressed from an intern through to worldwide head of sales and acquisitions, IMG Media, to president IMG Media and to his current role, alongside holding various board member positions and advisory roles.

LISA MASTERALEXIS (page 86)

Lisa Masteralexis is associate dean of Faculty & Administration, Isenberg School of Management, and Associate Professor, Mark H. McCormack Department of Sport Management, University of Massachusetts, Amherst.

BRECK McCORMACK (pages 116, 130, 193, 198, 211, 213 and 233)

Breck McCormack is Mark McCormack's son, and director of WineVine.tv. Previously, he was managing director, Asia at IMG.

CHRIS McCORMACK (pages 89 and 209)

Chris McCormack is Mark McCormack's grandson and an agent at TEAM8.

LESLIE McCORMACK GATHY (pages 48, 78, 94, 125, 140, 155 and 179)

Leslie McCormack Gathy is Mark McCormack's daughter and deputy chair, Right to Play UK. Previously, she was a senior international vice president, IMG.

TODD McCORMACK (pages 83 and 136)

Todd McCormack is Mark McCormack's son and senior corporate vice president, IMG. In addition, he serves as an adviser to and investor in a number of digital media companies.

PETER McKELVEY (pages 67, 155 and 236)

Peter McKelvey is president of the Americas, L.E.K. Consulting, a firm specialising in corporate strategy development and merger and acquisition advisory services. He joined in 1991 after receiving his MBA from The Wharton School.

SEAN McMANUS (pages 62 and 147)

Sean McManus is chairman of CBS Sports. Previous roles have included senior vice president, Programming at TWI (IMG's television production and distribution subsidiary), and president of both CBS Sports and CBS News.

COLIN MONTGOMERIE (pages 35 and 46)

Colin Montgomerie is a professional golfer and winning Ryder Cup Captain. He has won over 40 tournaments around the world, including the Senior PGA Championship, and was Europe's number one player for an unprecedented run of seven years.

MASAAKI MORITA (page 144)

Masaaki Morita is chairman, Masaaki Morita Tennis Fund, and honorary president, Japan Tennis Association. Previously he was chairman and president, Sony Life Insurance, and president and CEO, Sony Corporation of America.

JACK NICKLAUS (page 14)

Jack Nicklaus is a professional golfer, winner of a record eighteen professional major championship titles and 120 pro tournaments worldwide. He has been honoured with both the Congressional Gold Medal and the Presidential Medal of Freedom.

GEORGE O'GRADY (pages 23 and 223)

George O'Grady was CEO of the European Tour.

JEREMY PALMER-TOMKINSON (pages 64, 71, 117, 135, 180 and 224)

Jeremy Palmer-Tomkinson was senior vice president, event management, IMG.

ANDY PIERCE (pages 76, 80 and 204)

Andy Pierce is CEO, Americas and president of Golf & Consulting, Lagardère Sports and Entertainment. He has previously been managing director of consulting and senior corporate vice president, IMG.

JENI ROSE (pages 58, 181, 186 and 225)

Jeni Rose is vice president, IMG Models.

MELCOLM RUFFIN (page 98)

Melcolm Ruffin is an alumnus, Mark H. McCormack Department of Sport Management, University of Massachusetts and founder of the McCormack Sport Management Career Fair, University of Massachusetts.

KEN SCHOFIELD (pages 152 and 237)

Ken Schofield was executive director of the European Tour.

MONICA SELES (pages 33 and 229)

Monica Seles is a former world number one tennis player and winner of nine Grand Slam singles titles.

CATHERINE SIMPSON (pages 177 and 187)

Catherine Simpson is vice president, head of IPL Media and Events, IMG.

JOHN SKIPPER (pages 105 and 228)

John Skipper is ESPN president and co-chairman, Disney Media Networks. His previous roles include executive vice president, Content, at ESPN and a variety of roles within ESPN and The Walt Disney Company.

SIR MARTIN SORRELL (pages 164, 168 and 240)

Sir Martin Sorrell is CEO of WPP, and a former employee of IMG.

TIM SULLIVAN (pages 66, 137 and 139)

Tim Sullivan is president emeritus of The College of William and Mary, Virginia.

GARY SWAIN (pages 194 and 212)

Gary Swain is senior vice president, IMG.

FENG TAO (page 218)

Feng Tao is CEO of Shankai Sports.

LYNTON TAYLOR (pages 17 and 176)

Lynton Taylor has held a variety of positions including president and CEO Nine Network International, managing director IMG Media (TWI) Australia/NZ, chairman and managing director PBL Productions, and managing director World Series Cricket.

IAN TODD (pages 19, 23, 47, 62, 84, 113, 129, 137, 149 and 230)

Ian Todd is former president IMG International and former vice president, global sports marketing, Nike.

VIRGINIA WADE OBE (page 39)

Virginia Wade is a former professional tennis player, winner of three Grand Slam singles titles and four doubles titles, and was ranked number one in Great Britain for more than ten years. She is a tennis commentator for the BBC and Eurosport as well as for channels in the US.

CAROLINE WARD (pages 51, 53, 61 and 156)

Caroline Ward worked for IMG for 36 years, starting as a PA in Client Financial Services and rising to become senior vice president, Human Resources – International.

CASEY WASSERMAN (pages 178 and 229)

Casey Wasserman is chairman and CEO of Wasserman, a sports, entertainment and lifestyle marketing and management agency. He headed Los Angeles' Olympic host efforts as the LA2024 chairman, following which Los Angeles was selected to be the US Olympic bid city. He is also president and CEO of the Wasserman Foundation.

SARAH WOOLDRIDGE (pages 84 and 92)

Sarah Wooldridge is VIP Golf Events, Literary and Broadcasting, IMG. She first started working for IMG in 1966, as Mark McCormack's PA.

MICHAEL WRIGHT (pages 60, 72, 118 and 231)

Michael Wright is CEO of TWS (The Wright Stuff), a private sports consulting firm in Portland, Oregon. He was formerly managing director of IMG Canada and senior vice president in Corporate Consulting, Motorsports and Olympics.

SAM ZUSSMAN (page 161)

Sam Zussman is president of the IMG/WME events businesses, and also oversees the company's sports training division, IMG Performance.